For Aspiring

Court Interpreters

A Guide to Walk You Through the Steps
Toward Certification and Prepare You
to Pass the Written Exam

First Edition

Sandra Haydee Giroux

Disclaimer

This book is intended for educational and informational purposes only. It is designed to support aspiring court interpreters in developing their understanding of language usage, courtroom terminology, ethical standards, and basic criminal justice concepts. The content reflects the author's experience as a Florida state-certified court interpreter and as an educator.

The author is not a licensed attorney, and this book does not provide legal advice or guidance on courtroom procedures beyond general reference. While care has been taken to ensure the accuracy and relevance of the material, users of this book should consult official sources or certified legal professionals when seeking authoritative legal interpretation or advice.

All examples, scenarios, and commentary are intended to illustrate concepts and should not be relied upon as substitutes for professional training, certification requirements, or jurisdiction-specific regulations.

ISBN: 979-8-9930101-5-1

Copyright & Distribution Notice

Dedication

To the aspiring interpreter—this book is a companion for your calling.

To the One who whispered the words into my heart—I dedicate every page to You.

Acknowledgments

I extend heartfelt gratitude to **Prof. Karen Borgenheimer, MFA,** Director of the Translation & Interpreting Program at Florida International University, whose leadership and dedication to interpreter education inspired key facets of this work.

Special thanks to **Mrs. Mary Aponte,** Certified Court Interpreter and mentor to aspiring court interpreters, for her thoughtful review of my manuscript and her continued commitment to excellence in our field.

With gratitude to **Mrs. Janice Mudgett, BLS, MEd**—retired Media Specialist, wife, mother, grandmother, and believer—for her thoughtful review and gentle wisdom throughout this process.

I am also deeply grateful to **the legal expert** who generously reviewed the criminal justice section. Their careful insights helped ensure accuracy and integrity, enriching the legal context and affirming the ethical framework that guides interpreters in courtroom settings.

With appreciation to Microsoft Copilot for its invaluable assistance in developing ethics scenarios and reference materials.

Contents

Introduction

A Personal Welcome and Shared Purpose

You're here because you're curious, capable, and ready to make a difference. Whether you're just starting to explore interpreting or have already stepped into the courtroom, this book is for you. My goal is simple: to help you initiate the process of becoming a certified court interpreter, ensuring clarity, confidence and direction throughout, and to share insights I've gathered through two decades of experience in language services and education.

Since I reside in Florida, the certification steps and criminal justice concepts outlined in this book are fully aligned with Florida's standards. These may vary from state to state; however, the general and legal vocabulary, courtroom protocol, and ethical scenarios presented are broadly applicable in courtrooms across the United States.

The Need and the Challenge

In courtrooms across the United States, the demand for qualified interpreters is surging. Interpreter hours billed by state courts have risen by 30% over the past five years, reflecting a growing population of individuals with limited English proficiency (LEP) who rely on interpreters to access justice. Yet despite this need, becoming a certified court interpreter remains a rigorous process: passing rates for the written exam hover around 20–30%, while the oral exam—which tests simultaneous, consecutive, and sight translation skills—has a national pass rate of just 6–15%, depending on the state and language. These numbers underscore both the urgency of the role, and the high standards required to serve in it.

What You Stand to Gain

As of 2025, freelance certified court interpreters in Florida who work with agencies can earn up to $ 100 per hour, for English/Spanish assignments, the most in-demand language. For languages of lesser diffusion, rates often exceed this range. Assignments are billed in two-hour minimum blocks, making each engagement a meaningful opportunity. Work is consistent and on demand, and you don't need to advertise your services. Once your name is on the official registry of each state's office that handles court certification and regulation, you will be called for assignments.

For those pursuing stability as certified staff court interpreters, accurate and up-to-date salary information is available on the page titled *How Much Do Court Interpreters Make?*—located in the dropdown menu of my website, www.linguamia.com. Please note that salaries vary by judicial circuit.

Whether freelance or salaried, certified interpreters gain access to consistent work, professional credibility, and the opportunity to serve a vital role in the justice system.

A Profession That Challenges and Inspires

Court interpreting is rarely routine. From criminal arraignments to family court hearings, every assignment offers new subject matter, legal nuance, and human story. You might interpret for a witness one day and assist in a sentencing the next—each experience sharpens your skills and broadens your perspective.

While the role can be demanding, its variety keeps your mind engaged and your professional growth constant. If you thrive on intellectual challenge and meaningful service, this career offers both in abundance.

Your Roadmap to Certification

In Florida and most other states, becoming a state-certified court interpreter is a process made up of different stages, and each one brings you closer to a fulfilling and respected career. You'll begin by completing an orientation workshop, which introduces key concepts, an overview of the career, and expectations. From there, you'll take the written exam, and an overall score of 80% or higher is required to advance.

The next major challenge is the oral exam, which evaluates your ability to interpret in real time in each of the three modes of interpreting: Sight Translation, Consecutive Interpreting, and Simultaneous Interpreting. It begins with sight translation, where you're asked to read silently a written passage in English and translate it aloud in the target language, and vice versa. The consecutive mode consists of approximately 20 minutes of witness testimony. This section of the exam requires you to listen, take notes, and then interpret the speaker's message into the target language during pauses. Finally, the simultaneous component presents a continuous recording in English, which you must interpret into the target language without stopping, a skill that demands both accuracy and stamina. Each section reflects the real-world demands of the courtroom and measures your readiness to perform under pressure.

The minimum score on the oral exam is 70%. The final step is applying for Florida court interpreter registration, a process that involves court observation hours, a background check completed within three months of submission, and the appropriate non-refundable fee. Other states may have different classifications. Please, check the equivalence with your state's court interpreting regulatory entity.

While registration can occur after passing the written exam, I recommend waiting until you've passed the oral exam to ensure your momentum carries through.

Facing the Written Exam with Confidence

This book is designed to help you prepare thoroughly for the written exam, often the first major hurdle on the path to certification. I didn't pass it on my first attempt—at the time, even basic criminal justice concepts were unfamiliar to me, and like many aspiring interpreters, I had to study on my own. The vocabulary section includes sophisticated and nuanced terms that can only be mastered by immersing yourself in a wide variety of reading materials.

You'll be guided through each section of the test—from mastering advanced vocabulary and understanding court-related terms and usage, to applying proper professional ethics in complex scenarios. Through targeted exercises, insider strategies, basic legal concepts, and real-world examples, you'll gain the tools you need to feel confident in your foundational knowledge as you advance toward becoming a certified interpreter.

Preparation for the Oral Examination

While this book focuses primarily on written exam preparation, I would be remiss not to mention the oral exam, which requires consistent, targeted practice. To succeed, you must train daily across the three modes of interpretation: sight translation, consecutive, and simultaneous. I recommend practicing at least 30 minutes a day, five days a week—though during my own preparation, I dedicated about two hours every weekday. These skills are not acquired passively; they require intensive mental conditioning over a period of at least three months, with six months or more being ideal.

I didn't pass the oral exam on my first attempt either. My professional background was rooted in teaching, and I had not yet developed the interpreting stamina and reflexes needed to succeed. But once you begin to master these modes, something remarkable happens—your brain starts to crave the challenge. Interpreting sharpens your focus, deepens your linguistic agility, and before long, you'll find yourself growing more confident and proficient with each session.

Training Resources to Help You Succeed

To prepare for the oral exam, I strongly recommend investing in a specialized training program. Several reputable schools offer direct, targeted instruction to help you build the oral skills required for certification. Among them are De La Mora Institute, Interpretrain, Interpretools, Transinterpreting, Acebo, Interpreter Translation, LLC, and Castillo Language Services (Federal exam), each with its own approach to developing interpreting proficiency.

In addition, several universities offer certificate programs for aspiring interpreters, including Florida International University (FIU), the University of Central Florida (UCF), and the Middlebury Institute of International Studies at Monterey, California. These academic programs provide structured coursework and professional guidance to support your journey. You may also discover other valuable options online that align with your schedule and learning style.

Why I Wrote This Book

My passion for mentorship began early in my career as a staff interpreter, when I launched a community program to uplift aspiring interpreters.

My background in education consistently fueled my desire to raise awareness about this profession and to support recruitment efforts within both my judicial circuit and the wider justice system.

I was especially encouraged by my coworker at the time, Ms. Milena Clark, whose enthusiasm and support were a powerful motivator.

The pandemic brought those efforts to a halt—but not to an end. I continued mentoring individuals, one-on-one within my judicial circuit, even as I faced a personal challenge: two surgeries to remove a grapefruit-sized goiter lodged against one of my lungs. Although the procedure was successful, it left the muscle of one of my vocal cords permanently paralyzed.

Despite limited vocal strength, and thanks to the support of my judicial circuit supervisors, I developed a nationwide Zoom-based pilot program. But when my voice remained only half strong, I made the difficult decision to postpone the launch.

A Mentor Remembered, A Mission Reimagined

As I searched for a co-instructor to help launch the Zoom program, my thoughts returned to Mary Aponte, the certified court interpreter who first inspired me, a mentor and recruiter during my time teaching Spanish at the University of Tampa. While our styles and formats have grown in different directions over time, Mary has remained a constant guide to prospective court interpreters—her dedication, unwavering. Her influence helped shape the career I've grown to love. With her support and collaboration, we redesigned the pilot program to span just under five months. But as time went on, it became clear: with only one functioning vocal cord, teaching and interpreting were no longer sustainable. That realization gave rise to a new question—how else could I keep mentoring? The answer was simple: *I could write*. Through this book, I continue the mission to guide others and help aspiring court interpreters see their dream fulfilled with the understanding that every interpreter eventually finds their own voice and becomes a mentor in their own right.

Honoring Those Who Lifted Me

I also want to recognize Ms. Dianne Tornay, my coworker at the county where I eventually relocated. Dianne was more than a colleague—she was a mentor, and a trusted partner in reflection. Together, we debriefed the challenges we faced and supported each other in growing as professionals.

I'm equally grateful to my immediate supervisor, Mr. Juan Carlos Villanueva, whose exceptional leadership, unwavering support, and thoughtful guidance helped our circuit's programs flourish—including the mentorship initiative that sparked this book. His influence deeply shaped both my professional path and my personal growth.

While working at the Fifth Judicial Circuit, I had the privilege of receiving crucial support from Mrs. Stephanie Lorich, my supervisor's supervisor. Her encouragement was instrumental in helping me launch the mentorship program, laying the groundwork for what continues to be a resource for aspiring court interpreters.

Though I retired from my role as a staff interpreter, my commitment to mentoring never paused. I remain active in guiding prospective interpreters with the professional standards that fueled the original launch.

It's in that spirit of perseverance, gratitude, and giving back that I wrote this book—so others can rise with clarity, support, and purpose.

Chapter 1: Steps to Certification

In Florida, the official source for comprehensive information on becoming a certified court interpreter is www.flcourts.gov. Once on the homepage, navigate to "Services" in the top menu, select "Court Services", then "Court Interpreting." On that page, you'll find a menu on the right-hand side with links detailing procedures, requirements, and relevant forms for court interpreters. While I'll summarize the key steps in this book, the official website provides complete and up-to-date details. If you reside in another state, please locate the equivalent office that regulates court interpreter certification in your jurisdiction, where you'll find the most accurate requirements and calendar of events.

1.1 The Orientation Workshop

The first step toward becoming a certified court interpreter is to attend an orientation workshop provided by the Court Interpreter Certification and Regulation Program (CICRP). As the governing body for certification, CICRP oversees all official events, testing dates, and requirements. The orientation is held remotely over two full days, from 9:00 a.m. to 5:00 p.m., and must be completed before taking the exams. CICRP posts its calendar of events twice a year, so it's important to register early to secure a seat.

To register, fill out the required forms listed on the CICRP webpage: the Registration Form, Criminal Background Check and Good Moral Character Evaluation Acknowledgement, and Oath of Attendance. Submit these along with the workshop fee (payable by cashier's check or money order). Once your registration is processed, you'll receive a confirmation email with further in-structions.

1.2 About the Written Exam

After completing the orientation workshop, your next step is to ac-cess the Written Exam Information link located at the top right corner of the CICRP webpage. This section contains essential de-tails about the first certification exam, which is the central focus of this book. While we'll delve into the exam preparation here, it's important to review the entire webpage carefully, as it outlines critical content areas: general English proficiency, court-related terminology and usage, and professional ethics and conduct. You'll also find sample questions in this book to guide your study.

Unlike the orientation workshop, the written exam doesn't follow a set calendar. Once you're confident with the material, you may register online, complete the necessary form, and sub-mit the fee as instructed. The exam is computer based, allowing you to choose your preferred date and location—and you'll re-ceive results within 24 hours.

This book draws directly from CICRP's official study materials and additional resources listed in the bibliography. The selected terminology and sample questions were carefully curated to re-flect the format and content of the actual exam, with particular attention to what court interpreters most need to succeed.

1.3 Registering for the Written Exam

Once you're ready to take the written exam, visit the designated CICRP webpage and follow the registration instructions. Start by completing the Written Exam Oath and mailing it to CICRP's official address. Be sure to use the last five digits of your Social Security number as your test ID when filling out the form.

Next, use the Online Written Exam Portal link on the same page to register. If this is your first time taking the exam, you'll need to create new login credentials. Before approving your registration, CICRP will verify two key requirements: that your Written Exam Oath has been received, and that you completed the Orientation Workshop within the past three years.

Once these are confirmed, you'll receive an email from CICRP with instructions to proceed. You can then select your exam date, time, and location, and submit your payment through the vendor's website. This final step is completed online.

If you have a disability recognized under the Americans with Disabilities Act (ADA), be sure to request special accommodations in advance. All other required registration forms should be completed and mailed to the CICRP office address listed on the official website along with the appropriate fee in the form of a money order.

A more in-depth look at the written exam will follow in a subsequent section.

1.4 Maintaining Certification

To maintain your registration or certification designation in Florida, interpreters must meet several biennial requirements. These include completing 16 hours of Continuing Interpreting Education (CIEs), with at least two credits focused on ethics. Once you obtain registered status, your name will be listed on a registry published on your state's official website and included in your state's database for updates on approved Continuing Interpreter Education classes you can take.

You must also fulfill 20 law-related professional interpreting assignments, or alternatively, a smaller number of assignments totaling no fewer than 40 hours.

Renewal requires submitting the Court Interpreter Registration Renewal application along with a $200 fee (as of 2025), and this process must be completed every two years.

Requirements may vary by state, so be sure to consult your local Office of Language Access to confirm the specific guidelines that apply to your jurisdiction.

1.5 Designation Levels **(from basic to advanced)**

Registered Only Status

The most basic designation for court interpreters is Registered Only status. You may obtain this designation by applying after passing either the written exam or the oral exam. Once approved, your name is added to the official registry maintained by the Office of the State Courts Administrator (OSCA), which serves as a public resource for locating qualified interpreters. In Florida, you can access this registry and other language access resources through the Florida Courts website. If you're outside Florida, check with your state's equivalent office for interpreter registration and certification guidelines.

During the first year of every two-year registration period, interpreters holding Registered Only Status must complete at least one of the following assessments, depending on their language and designation: a full oral performance examination, an abbreviated oral performance examination, or an oral proficiency interview (OPI).

If you obtain employment as a staff interpreter with this designation, you need to become certified within one year of beginning employment, unless modified in exceptional circumstances.

To apply for registration-only status, you need to fill out an application, along with an accompanying document, complete your observation hours, and send payment. All mailed to the respective office. Please, refer to your official state's website for specific instructions and documents.

Provisionally Approved Designation

You may be granted Provisionally Approved status if you achieve a minimum overall score of 65% on the full oral performance exam, with at least 60% on each individual section—sight translation, consecutive, and simultaneous interpretation. This designation is valid for two years and cannot be renewed. It serves as a transitional status, allowing interpreters to continue gaining experience while working toward full certification. To retain eligibility, you must become certified within that two-year window; otherwise, the designation will expire.

Language Skilled Designation

This designation is reserved only for languages in which there is no oral performance examination. Prospective court interpreters will pass an oral proficiency interview.

Certified Designation with Abbreviated Performance Examination

It is obtained with an abbreviated Oral Performance Examination which is offered in Bosnian/Serbian/Croatian and Turkish.

Certified Designation with a Full Oral Performance Examination

Full oral performance examinations in Florida are currently available in Amharic, Arabic, Cantonese, Filipino (Tagalog), French, Haitian Creole, Hmong, Khmer, Korean, Mandarin, Polish, Portuguese, Russian, Spanish, Somali, and Vietnamese.

Chapter 2: Structure of the Written Exam

The primary goal of this book is to prepare you to succeed on the written exam, so you can confidently move on to the Oral Performance Examination. The written exam consists of 135 multiple-choice questions and must be completed within two hours and fifteen minutes. The exam is structured as follows:

- Part I: General English Language Proficiency — 75 multiple-choice questions

- Part II: Court-Related Terms & Usage, and Ethics & Professional Conduct — 60 multiple-choice questions

To pass, you must score at least 75% on each section, with a minimum overall score of 80%. Candidates may test up to three times per year, provided the same version of the exam is not retaken more than once in a six-month period.

This book mirrors the exam format provided by the CICRP office, offering practice materials and terminology most relevant to court interpreters. Its aim is to help you build familiarity with the structure and confidently approach each section.

You may purchase full-length practice exams for the written test from the author's website or other reputable vendors. If you choose to do so, you can apply the following grading guidelines provided by the CICRP office to assess your performance:

"...the examinee must answer a minimum of 57 out of 75 questions correctly on Part I, 45 out of 60 questions correctly on Part II, and answer 108 questions correctly overall in order to pass."

2.1 Part I: Vocabulary

The vocabulary portion of the written exam consists of five distinct sections: three focused on synonyms, one on antonyms, and one on idiomatic expressions. Because the majority of these sections emphasize synonyms, it's important to pay extra attention during the antonym portion—don't let the previous pattern influence your selections. In this chapter, we'll walk through one sample from each section to help build familiarity. Toward the end of the book, you'll also find a condensed version of a practice exam to reinforce what you've learned.

2.1.1 How to Study Vocabulary

Effective vocabulary study begins with thoughtful exploration. While you may discover strategies that work best for your own learning style, consider the following suggestions to build a strong foundation:

- Read widely and often: Dive into diverse subjects such as science, history, the environment, literature, and more. Explore editorials, academic journals, and trusted articles to encounter challenging vocabulary in context.

- Study test-specific word lists: Resources from standardized tests, such as the SAT, ACT, and TOEFL, can provide excellent vocabulary practice. If permitted, copy and paste online lists into your own document for easier review, rather than downloading files directly from unknown sources. You may also find quality vocabulary books—new or used—that serve as valuable tools.

- If flashcards work for you, great! If not, consider using vocabulary apps that allow you to create your own glossaries. One example is *Kalimaty*, which I personally enjoy for its ability to organize glossaries by category and continuously add new words as I encounter them, and it is free as long as I use only words, no images.

- For idiom practice, I recommend reviewing *In the Loop*, the idiom dictionary posted under the study materials section of the written exam on the official CICRP website. Another helpful resource is *The Idiom Connection* at idiomconnection.com.

- To study words in context, explore any artificial intelligence platform by entering a prompt with your vocabulary list, then read and analyze how the terms are used. Some examples include: *Copilot by Microsoft*, *ChatGPT by OpenAI*, *Gemini by Google*, *Claude by Anthropic*, and *Meta AI*. These tools can give you dynamic, real-time examples and help reinforce nuanced language use.

  As an example, here's a prompt I used on one of the AI platforms to explore vocabulary in context:

  "Create a short story using the following words: coddle, patronize, flamboyant, arcane, flout, protean, and inimical."

  And AI created this story:

  "In the bustling city of Eldoria, where the rich patronized the poor and the ambitious flouted tradition, there lived a <u>flamboyant</u> scholar named Lucian. He was a man of <u>protean</u> talents, shifting effortlessly between disciplines that most found <u>arcane</u>. Some called him a genius; others found his endless reinvention <u>inimical</u> to the established order.

Lucian had long tired of being <u>coddled</u> by admirers who sought only to bask in his intellect without truly challenging it. And so, when the Grand Academy invited him to lecture, he did not offer dry theories or polite discourse. Instead, he turned the lecture hall into a whirlwind of ideas, tearing down sacred assumptions with a wicked grin.

The elders scoffed, their rigid minds resisting change. But in the back row, a young woman named Callista listened—her eyes alight with revelation. She had spent years trying to understand the <u>arcane</u> texts locked away in the Academy's archives, and for the first time, she saw a path forward.

When the lecture ended, Callista approached Lucian. 'Teach me,' she said simply.

Lucian chuckled. 'Only if you promise never to let me <u>coddle</u> you.'

She smiled. 'Only if you promise never to <u>patronize</u> me.'

And so began a mentorship that would shake Eldoria to its foundations."

(M.S. Copilot)

This type of exercise not only reinforces meaning through usage but also sparks creativity by connecting abstract or challenging words in a narrative form.

2.2 Vocabulary Sections with Examples. The directions follow the model of the written exam created by the National Center for State Courts (NCSC).

Section 1: Sentence Completion

This section consists of unfinished sentences. Please select from the list of four words or phrases (A, B, C, D) the option that best completes the sentence.

Example: In 1865, the Thirteenth Amendment ____ slavery.

A. established

B. overlooked

C. abolished

D. abhorred

(C is the best answer)

Section 2: Synonyms in Context

This section consists of sentences that contain an underlined word or phrase. Please choose from a list of four words or phrases (A, B, C, D) the option that is closest in meaning to the underlined word or phrase.

Example: The sophisticated electronic equipment enables the helicopter to operate well at night.

A. sensationalist

B. enjoyable

C. comfortable

D. advanced

(D is the best answer)

Section 3: Synonyms

This section consists of words or phrases. Please select from the list of four words or phrases (A, B, C, or D) the one that has the same meaning or closest to the same meaning as the word or phrase provided.

Example: buttress

A. support

B. stone

C. undercut

D. steel

(A is the best answer)

Section 4: Antonyms

Please select from a list of four words or phrases the option that is most opposite in meaning to the word or phrase provided.

Example: severe

A. opposite

B. moderate

C. dissociated

D. foggy

(B is the best answer)

<u>Section 5: Idioms</u>

This section consists of sentences that contain an underlined idiomatic expression. Please select from the list of four words or phrases the option that is closest in meaning to the underlined idiom.

Example: I am not sure what to believe when Zena speaks about Marcelo. She has had <u>a grudge</u> since Marcelo did not show up at her graduation even though he had promised that he would be there for her.

A. an ace in the hole

B. an albatross around his neck

C. all thumbs

D. ax to grind

(D is the best answer)

2.3 Key Points

- Vocabulary sections consist of synonyms, synonyms in context, sentence completion, antonyms, and idioms.
- You need to read a variety of sources extensively.

Sandra Haydee Giroux

Chapter 3: Part II: Court-Related Terms and Usage, Ethics and Professional Conduct

3.1 Court-Related Terms and Usage. Key Concepts and Procedures

To understand court-related terminology and its proper usage, it's essential to first grasp how criminal justice procedures work. In this chapter, we'll cover foundational knowledge designed to help you pass the written exam with confidence. While owning a criminal justice textbook can be helpful, I've curated key concepts and terms for you—many of which were drawn from the official glossary for interpreters posted on Florida's court website. Now, let's turn our attention to the terms and procedures that matter most at this stage.

Because I am not a lawyer, certain passages are quoted verbatim to reflect the source material with complete accuracy.

Terms underlined within the paragraphs represent key vocabulary you'll need to know.

In any state there are both state and federal courts. As a nation we have the Constitution of the United States, and each state has its own constitution which outlines the specific powers, duties and rights of citizens within each state.

The U.S. court systems—both federal and state—are organized in a hierarchical structure. In Florida, the lowest level is the county court. Above it are the circuit courts, totaling 20 across the state. Next are the District Courts of Appeal, comprising six appellate courts. At the top of the hierarchy is the Florida Supreme Court, which serves as the court of last resort.

The types of cases assigned to the various trial courts differ from state to state; the names of these trial courts also differ from state to state. In Florida, as an example, there are two types of trial courts: County and Circuit. In Florida, county courts resolve misdemeanor cases, most traffic offenses, and most civil cases where there is $50,000 or less in dispute. Circuit courts in Florida resolve felony cases, family law cases, civil cases involving damages over $50,000 and most other legal disputes.

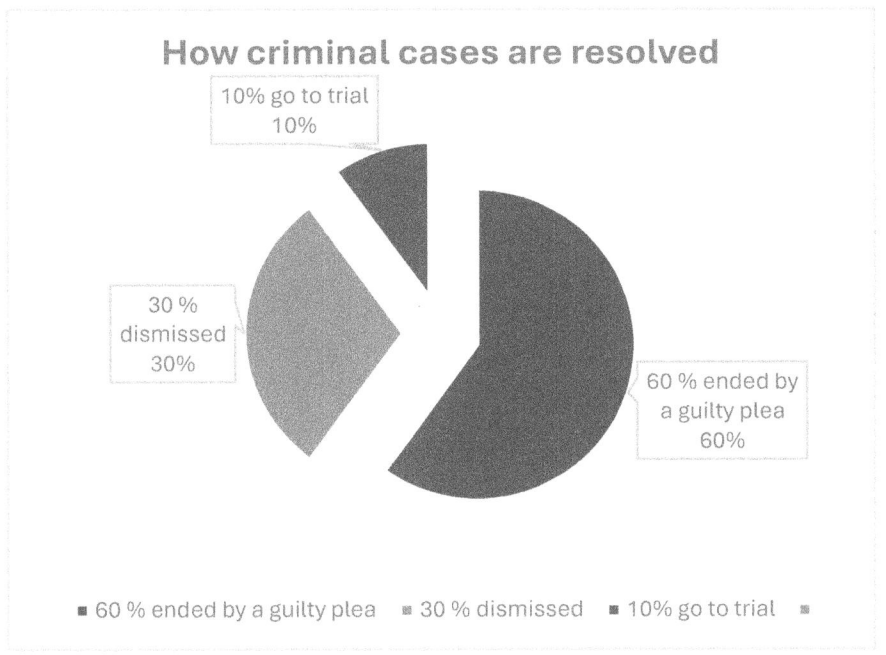

How criminal cases are resolved

10% go to trial
10%

30 % dismissed
30%

60 % ended by a guilty plea
60%

■ 60 % ended by a guilty plea   ■ 30 % dismissed   ■ 10% go to trial   ■

*This chart was taken from Law & the Courts, vol. 1, page 9
(This model, even though not the most recent, may reflect current per-
centages.)

3.2 The Criminal Justice System - Steps in Processing a Criminal Case - A General Outline

Our analysis begins with an overview of the criminal justice system. The customary steps in a criminal prosecution are as follows:

- The commission of a crime

- The report of a crime/ observation of a crime by law enforcement.

- The police then may conduct further investigation into criminal activity in order to gather evidence that can help identify a suspect and justify an arrest. Such investigation may involve searching a person or property. <u>For law enforcement to legally conduct a search, there must either be a search warrant issued by a judge authorizing such a search, or the search must otherwise be conducted pursuant to some recognized exception to this warrant requirement.</u>

- The police then have discretion to decide whether to conduct an <u>arrest</u> of a suspect based on their investigation or based upon their own knowledge and observations. The arrested individual (now named a Defendant in the resulting criminal prosecution) will either be taken into custody, or given a notice to appear for a later court date. *Probable cause* <u>is the legal standard required for law enforcement to conduct an arrest</u>. <u>Probable cause means that law enforcement has a reasonable basis to believe a crime has occurred, and the defendant is the person who committed that crime.</u>

- <u>Booking</u>: Following arrest, the defendant will be taken into custody and transported to a local jail or detention center, for what is commonly referred to as *booking*. Booking refers to the process in which personal information about an arrested criminal suspect is recorded in a police station or jail system. In addition to gathering personal details, this process includes taking fingerprints and <u>mugshots</u> (photographs) and searching the suspect's personal belongings.

- After booking, the defendant may have an opportunity to immediately post bond/bail and be released from custody pending a future court date, or the defendant may possibly remain in custody until an initial or preliminary hearing is conducted before a judge, which usually occurs within 24 hours of arrest, depending on the jurisdiction in which the crime occurs.

- Initial/preliminary hearing before a judge will then take place for defendants who remain in custody post-arrest. At this hearing, the presiding judge will determine whether probable cause existed to justify the defendant's arrest, whether they qualify for a court-appointed attorney to be assigned to their case (usually referred to as a *public defender*) and what the amount of any bond/bail will be (<u>bond/bail being synonymous terms referring to the amount of money, determined by the judge or by applicable law, which has to be paid into the court system before the defendant will be eligible for release</u>, customarily required to ensure the defendant will return for future court dates). The judge may also set conditions to govern the conduct of any defendant released from custody pursuant to posting bond/bail and release from custody.

- Next, the court will set the case for an <u>arraignment</u>. The arraignment is a court proceeding in which the court informs the defendant of their constitutional rights, advises the defendant of the charges that have been filed by the prosecuting authority, and offers the defendant an opportunity to enter a plea (the defendant may plead guilty, not guilty, or no contest).

- The prosecution of a criminal defendant is then carried out by the prosecuting authority (usually a State Attorney or a District Attorney at the state level, or an Assistant U.S. Attorney at the federal level). These prosecutors represent the government, whether at the state or federal level, in criminal cases. When deciding whether to charge an individual with a crime, prosecutors consider several factors, including the seriousness of the offense, the strength of the evidence, and the interests of the alleged victim(s). Charges are then filed either by what is called an *indictment* or by what is called an *information*. (For more details on this process, please refer to the section titled "The Prosecution and the Defense,"

- Indictment is a formal written criminal charge presented by a grand jury. This document initiates the formal criminal process against a defendant, regularly for serious offenses. It involves crimes punishable with imprisonment. The standard is probable cause. It is conducted in a closed hearing, no defense attorney or defendant present. Used by the federal government and about half the states.

- Information is also a formal written charge, usually filed by a state prosecutor; this charging document outlines the specific crimes the defendant is accused of. It involves crimes punishable with imprisonment. The standard is also probable cause. Both defense attorney and defendant can be present.

- There are other ways in which a criminal case may begin, including criminal *complaints* by alleged victims to a prosecuting authority, and the filing of other types of charging documents with the court, such as *notices to appear* and *criminal citations* issued by law enforcement, which customarily do not involve an arrest but simply advise the defendant of the offense alleged and a court date to appear for an arraignment.

- Following arraignment, the defendant will be required to attend a number of pre-trial court hearings (the number of which differ from state-to-state and judge-to-judge) at which the prosecutor and the defendant's defense attorney will address any legal matters with the presiding judge that require resolution prior to a trial.

- Discovery is often conducted by the prosecutor and defense attorney, which include conducting depositions of material witnesses and exchanging relevant evidence that might be used at trial by either party or which otherwise must be disclosed by the party in possession of that evidence.

- Motion practice may also take place, in which the prosecutor and defense attorney file various legal motions with the court, seeking a favorable ruling from the judge on important legal issues that can affect how the case will proceed, or how the evidence may be presented at trial.

- Plea bargaining or charge bargaining will also take place between the defense attorney and the prosecutor in an effort to resolve the case. Usually, in plea bargaining, the defendant agrees to plead guilty in exchange for the prosecutor recommending a particular sentence to be imposed by the judge, whereas charge bargaining involves the defendant agreeing to plead guilty and accepting sentence in exchange for the prosecutor reducing or dismissing certain charges.

- <u>Trial</u> – If the case does not resolve through such bargaining or through motion practice, the case is set for a trial. The trier of fact is either a judge (bench trial, adversary) or a jury (jury trial, adversary). A prosecutor and a defense attorney participate in the proceeding. In <u>criminal trials the standard of proof for criminal conviction is</u> <u>*proof beyond and to the exclusion of a reasonable doubt*</u>. That means, if there is some reasonable doubt (not merely speculation or conjecture that results in some doubt about the guilt of the defendant) then the defendant should be found to be not guilty and acquitted by the <u>trier of fact</u>. In <u>civil trials, the standard of proof for one party to prevail over another is the *preponderance of the evidence*, meaning the trier of fact must determine whether the greater weight of the evidence favors the plaintiff or defendant.</u>

- <u>In a civil case, the trier of fact will customarily award damages to the prevailing party, as financial compensation. In a criminal case, sentencing</u> by a judge will take place should the defendant be found guilty by the trier of fact. Possible criminal sentences include:

- A fine

- Probation

- Incarceration in a jail or prison

- Some combination of supervision in the community and incarceration

  ➤ A <u>Presentence Investigation Report (PSI)</u> is needed when a defendant is found guilty. It is usually

> prepared by a probation officer after a guilty plea or conviction, and before the sentencing hearing.
>
> ➢ See additional information in chapter 3, section 3.10.1 Sentencing.

- <u>Appeals</u>: Should the defendant wish to challenge their guilty verdict in a criminal case, or should either party in a civil case wish to challenge the verdict in their trial, an appeal is filed. They are filed by attorneys in the <u>appellate courts</u> and then ruled on by <u>appellate judges</u>. "If an appellate court reverses a case, the case returns to trial court for retrial. With a reversal, the original trial becomes <u>moot</u> (that is, it is as though it never happened). Following the reversal, a prosecutor decides whether to refile or to drop the charges. Even if the prosecutor drops the charges, the defendant can still be prosecuted later as long as the statute of limitations for the crime the defendant is accused of committing hasn't run out. Such a statute imposes time limits on the government to try a case." (*CliffsNotes online on Criminal Justice: The major steps in processing a criminal case*)

- <u>Release</u>: Any defendant sentenced to incarceration will ultimately be granted release, either by serving the maximum term of imprisonment or by means of an early release procedure, such as <u>parole</u> or <u>pardon</u>.

- **Parole**: The temporary release of a <u>prisoner</u> (for a special purpose) or permanent release before the completion of a sentence, on the promise of good behavior.

- **Pardon:** "A pardon is forgiveness by the governor for a crime committed. A person who is pardoned cannot be further punished for the forgiven offense and should not be penalized for having a record of the offense." (*lasclev.org*)

3.3 Citizens' Rights

3.3.1 The Bill of Rights

The Bill of Rights, made up of the first ten amendments to the U.S. Constitution, forms the core of citizens' rights, and was enacted in 1791. It defines certain rights of the American people and limitation upon the government to prevent the violation of these rights. Some of the amendments relate directly to criminal justice.

- **Fourth Amendment**: The government may not conduct _unreasonable searches and seizures_ under the Fourth Amendment. It requires warrants to be based on _probable cause_, supported by oath or affirmation, and to specifically describe the place to be searched and the people or things to be seized.

- **Fifth Amendment:** Provides the privilege against self-incrimination, prohibits the government from trying a person twice for the same offense (double jeopardy), and promises _due process of law_.

- **Sixth Amendment**: The requirements for criminal trials, including the defendant's _right to counsel_, are set out in the Sixth Amendment.

- **Eighth Amendment** prohibits the government from inflicting _cruel and unusual punishment on prisoners_.

- Additionally, the **Fourteenth Amendment**, ratified in 1868, was added to the Constitution after the Civil War. It prohibits states from depriving any person of life, liberty, or property without *due process of law*.

3.3.2 The Fourth Amendment and the Exclusionary Rule

The exclusionary rule is a legal principle that prohibits using illegally obtained evidence in court. The Fourth Amendment, which protects citizens from unreasonable searches and seizures, is the source of this rule.

If evidence is obtained through an illegal search or seizure, without a warrant or probable cause or if a confession is coerced or interrogation is obtained without proper <u>Miranda rights</u>, then, that evidence cannot be used to convict a defendant in court.

If evidence, usually physical evidence, was obtained illegally, a <u>motion to suppress</u> that evidence can be filed, requesting the court to exclude it from the trial. This motion argues that the evidence violates the defendant's constitutional rights, particularly the Fourth Amendment's protection against unreasonable searches and seizures.

Examples of Physical Evidence:

Weapons, tools, notes, letters, papers, bullets, vehicles, cigarette butts, blood, semen, hair, tissue, saliva, urine, feces, vomit, fingerprints, tire tracks, footprints, palm prints, tool marks, bullet holes, damaged areas, dents, breaks, etc.

Police searches can be conducted with a warrant or, in certain circumstances, without a warrant.

Examples of Searches:

- Searching a home or other building for evidence based on a warrant issued by a judge specifying the place to be searched and items to be seized.

- Electronic eavesdropping. It consists of both telephone wiretapping and bugging.

- Search of a vehicle.

- Retrieval of electronic data, including emails and text messages, the GPS location of certain electronic devices, etc.

3.3.3 Case Law examples that Support the Exclusionary Rule

"*Kyllo v. United States*, 533 U.S. 27 (2001), was a decision by the Supreme Court of the United States in which the court ruled that the use of thermal imaging devices to monitor heat radiation in or around a person's home, even if conducted from a public vantage point, is unconstitutional without a search warrant..."

(Kyllo v. United States, Wikipedia)

"*Florida v. Jardines*, 569 U.S. 1 (2013), was a Supreme Court of the United States case in which it was ruled that police use of a trained detection dog to sniff for narcotics on the front porch of a private home is a 'search' within the meaning of the Fourth Amendment to the United States Constitution, and therefore, without consent, requires both probable cause and a search warrant". (Florida v. Jardines, Wikipedia)

3.3.4 The Miranda Rights

<u>Miranda rights</u>, often referred to as the "<u>Miranda warning</u>" is a set of rights that the police is required to read to a <u>suspect</u> who is <u>in custody</u> and <u>about to be interrogated</u>, according to a 1966 Supreme Court case, *Miranda v. Arizona,* 384 U.S. 436 (1966).

These rights ensure that individuals understand their constitutional protections while being questioned by law enforcement and protect their <u>Fifth Amendment right against self-incrimination</u> and <u>Sixth Amendment right to counsel</u>.

The Miranda warning typically includes:

➢ You have the right to remain silent.
➢ Anything you say can and will be used against you in a court of law.
➢ You have the right to have a lawyer present while you are being questioned.
➢ If you cannot afford to hire a lawyer, one will be provided to represent you.

In summary, the Miranda warning is required when a person <u>is in custody</u> and law enforcement <u>intends to interrogate them</u>.

Imagery that I use to remember this order is a sandwich: custody – Miranda rights – interrogation.

3.3.5 The Fifth Amendment: Right to Remain Silent

The Fifth Amendment generally applies to statements made to law enforcement, and directs that any statement made by a defendant must be freely and voluntarily given. Incriminating statements, where the defendant provides information or evidence that would tend to show their guilt, <u>cannot be compelled by law</u>

enforcement against the defendant's wishes. Thus, the Miranda warning discussed above is provided by law enforcement to advise the criminally accused of their right to remain silent and to refuse to answer such potentially incriminating questions by invoking their rights under the Fifth Amendment – commonly referred to as *Pleading the Fifth*. In general, the Fifth Amendment can also be invoked in civil proceedings.

In Summary, Key Situations Where an Individual Can Plead the Fifth:

- Police Interrogations:
  If a suspect is being questioned by law enforcement and believes their answers could lead to criminal charges, they can invoke their right to remain silent.

- Court Proceedings:
  As a defendant or a witness, an individual can decline to answer questions that could potentially incriminate them.

- Civil Cases:
  An individual can refuse to answer questions that could incriminate them in a civil lawsuit.

"However, there are limits. Individuals cannot invoke the Fifth Amendment if granted immunity, as their statements can no longer be used against them in a criminal prosecution. Similarly, those pardoned, convicted, and sentenced cannot invoke the Fifth Amendment regarding the same crime". *Andrew Cove, July 15, 2024*

3.4 Offenses and Crimes

3.4.1 Classification of Offenses

Put in a simplified way, crimes are generally classified into three categories: <u>felonies</u>, <u>misdemeanors</u>, and <u>infractions</u>.

Felonies

Felony offenses are the most serious types of crime. Upon conviction for a felony offense, the standard sentence for a convicted defendant is a term of imprisonment for more than one year to be served in a state or in a federal penitentiary; the standard sentence for misdemeanor offenses, being less serious crimes, is imprisonment for a year or less in duration, to be served in a local jail or detention facility.

In Florida, sentences for felonies can range from a year and a day in prison, to lifetime incarceration, or even capital punishment pursuant to the death penalty, depending on the gravity of the crime, the offender's prior criminal history, and other factors. Felonies are classified as first, second, and third degree, life felonies and capital felonies, depending on the severity of the crime.

Examples of Felonies:

- Robbery

- Murder

- Aggravated battery

- Child abuse

- Burglary

- Kidnapping

- Grand theft

- Incest

- Carjacking

- Drug trafficking

- Resisting an officer with violence

- Arson

- Sexual crimes

- Assault with a deadly weapon

- Aggravated battery

- Forgery

Misdemeanors

Misdemeanor offenses are considered less serious than felonies and are usually dealt with in a County Court. They are classified as first-degree and second-degree misdemeanors, and sentences vary depending on the degree.

First-degree misdemeanors carry a maximum sentence of up to a year in jail and a $1,000 fine, while second-degree misdemeanors can result in up to 60 days in jail and a $500 fine.

Examples of Misdemeanors in Florida (from floridacourtrecords.us)

Misdemeanors of the First Degree

- Theft (second or subsequent offenses, or first offense with over $100 in the value of stolen property)

- Vandalism, aka Criminal Mischief

- Indecent exposure

- Simple battery

- Marijuana possession (less than 20gm)

Misdemeanors of the Second Degree

- Simple assault

- Simple trespass

- Disorderly conduct

- Petit theft (first offense, less than $100 in the value of stolen property)

- Driving on a suspended license

Examples of Criminal Traffic Violations Include:

- Driving under the influence (DUI)

- Reckless driving

- Knowingly driving with a suspended license

- Leaving the scene of an accident with property damage

Infractions

Infractions, also called violations, are civil in nature, and involve the least serious offenses (such as jaywalking, and various motor vehicle offenses. Being civil in nature, infractions are not subject to any risk of incarceration but are generally punishable by a fine and perhaps the imposition of other sanctions, such as driver's education courses, the loss of driver's privileges, or the performance of community service.

Examples of Infractions

Examples of Infractions Are as Follows:

- Executing an illegal U-turn

- Trespassing

- Speeding over legal limits

- Driving without insurance or registration

- Disobeying a stop light

- Littering

- Illegal street crossing

- Driving without a seat belt

- Running a stop sign

- No child seat belt

3.5 Elements of a Crime

To determine criminal activity, two elements must be present:

3.5.1 Mens Rea

Mens rea is the Latin word for guilty mind, and refers to the criminal intent and mental state of the defendant at the time of the crime, and the defendant's ability to distinguish right from wrong.

3.5.2 Actus Reus

Actus reus is the actual action required for the commission of a crime. This action must be voluntary, intentional, and unlawful. However, even non-action can constitute as actus reus: "An omission can also constitute an actus reus if there is a legal duty to act. This means that not taking any action when legally obligated to do so can result in criminal liability. For example, if someone fails to report a crime they know about or fails to provide aid in an emergency, they could be found guilty of committing a criminal offense." (legal.thompsonreuters.com)

3.5.3 Concurrence of both Mens Rea and Actus Reus

Concurrence requires that both mens rea and actus reus must be present simultaneously before establishing any kind of legal accountability.

Summary

- Criminal activity requires both mens rea (criminal intent) and actus reus (criminal act).

- Actus reus is the physical action required for a crime and must be voluntary, intentional, and unlawful.

- Mens rea refers to the mental intent behind an act or omission and can include intentionality, recklessness, or negligence.

- Causation and concurrence are very important elements for criminal liability, with causation determining if an act caused harm and concurrence requiring both actus reus and mens rea to occur at the same time.

3.6 Sources of Criminal Law

Criminal law defines criminal offenses; sets out the procedures for arrest, search and seizure, and interrogation; lays down the rules for trials; and determines the penalties for offenders. What are the sources of criminal law?

3.6.1 The U.S. Constitution

The U.S. Constitution is the supreme law of the land, and all judges are bound by it. If any other laws conflict with the U.S. Constitution, the U.S. Supreme Court can rule them as unconstitutional. States create their own constitutions, and all local laws must comply with them.

3.6.2 State Constitutions

Each state has its own constitution, which generally allows for easier amendment than the U.S. Constitution. This reflects the specific interests and needs of each state's population over time. Their functions include:

- They define the three branches of the state government — legislative, executive and judicial — and their respective powers and functions.

- State constitutions often include their own versions of a Bill of Rights, detailing individual freedoms that may extend beyond federal protections. These can include specific rights relating to education, healthcare, or environmental protection.

- They provide the framework for setting up and running local government structures within the state.

- State constitutions establish the rules and limitations for how states can collect taxes and incur debt.

- They delineate the procedures by which the constitution itself may be amended or revised, which may encompass the legislature, a popular initiative, or a constitutional convention.

3.6.3 Statutes and Ordinances

Most criminal law is made up of laws passed by Congress and state legislatures. Each state and the federal government have a statutory criminal code. Laws that define crimes such as homicide, rape, and robbery are usually statutory. There is some overlap between state and federal statutes.

Ordinances, which form part of the criminal law, are enacted by municipal councils.

3.6.4 Case Law

Case law is law made by judges. It means that when a court makes a decision, that decision becomes precedent and governs other cases with similar legal issues.

See examples in section 3.3.3 Case Law examples.

3.6.5 Administrative Rules and Regulations

These rules and regulations are developed by U.S. government agencies and commissions. These agencies clarify how these rules and regulations are applied and enforced, investigate violations, and impose sanctions.

Examples of these violations are exporting without a license, income tax evasion, selling contaminated food, dumping toxic waste, etc.

Examples of agencies that make these rules are:

- The Food and Drug Administration (FDA)

- Internal Revenue Service (IRS)

- Environmental Protection Agency (EPA)

- The Federal Trade Commission (FTC)

- Department of Labor (DOL)

- U.S. Department of Education (ED)

- Department of Transportation (DOT)

- Etc.

It is estimated that there are over 400 federal agencies including independent regulatory bodies, government corporations, and executive departments.

3.7 The Prosecution and the Defense

According to the <u>adversarial model</u> of criminal justice, the best way to discover the truth is to have advocates for both the prosecution and the defense. The facts are to be presented by each advocate from a partisan point of view. The idea behind this system is to make sure that all the important facts and arguments are put before the person in charge of making the decision, <u>the fact-finder</u>: the jury in a <u>jury trial</u>, or the judge in a <u>bench trial</u>.

3.7.1 Prosecutors

Prosecutors represent the government in court. They work with law enforcement to bring cases to justice and present evidence against defendants in criminal courts. They investigate crimes and decide whether to file or dismiss charges.

The prosecutor may engage in plea bargaining.

A **nolle prosequi** is a formal declaration by the prosecutor that a case is being closed. Reasons for issuing a nolle prosequi (nol.pros.) include insufficient or inadmissible evidence; false accusations, and the trivial nature of some crimes.

When a prosecutor brings a case to trial, they are responsible for proving the defendant's guilt <u>beyond a reasonable doubt</u>. <u>The prosecutor bears the burden of proof in criminal cases.</u> The defendant, on the other hand, is presumed innocent until proven guilty.

Before trial, the prosecutor prepares evidence, interviews witnesses and victims, drafts motions and subpoenas. They also exchange information (<u>discovery</u>) with the defendant and/or their defense attorney, evidence that they intend to use at trial.

3.7.2 Types of Prosecutors

- **The U.S. Attorney General,** who is <u>the country's</u> chief law enforcement officer and the head of the Department of Justice. They are responsible for supervising U.S. attorneys.

  o U.S. Attorneys

*There is one for each of the 94 federal judicial districts in the United States which handle both civil and criminal matters.

*They are appointed by the president of the United States. They have assistant U.S. attorneys to help them handle cases.

*U.S. Attorneys often work together with state and local prosecutors.

- **The State Attorney General** is the <u>state</u> government's highest law enforcement officer.

  o State Attorneys (S.A.)/District Attorneys (D.A.) [In Florida: State Attorney]

  o They work at state, county and municipal levels of government.

3.7.3 The Defense Attorney

Their job is to defend their client's legal rights and ensure a fair trial by presenting a compelling defense, challenging the prosecution's evidence.

At trial, the defense presents an opening statement, presents evidence, calls witnesses, cross-examines witnesses, and delivers a closing argument to the jury.

The defense also may negotiate with the prosecution in order to reach a potential plea deal.

The goal in their closing arguments is to persuade the jury or judge that there is reasonable doubt about their client's guilt, resulting in an acquittal.

3.7.4 Types of Defense Attorneys

Public Defenders

Public defenders and their assistants are government-employed attorneys who represent defendants who cannot afford to hire a lawyer privately.

Private Attorneys

Private attorneys are hired by individuals or organizations to represent them in court.

3.8 The Pre-Trial Process

3.8.1 Pre-Trial Procedures in Civil Cases

In civil proceedings the person filing the complaint is referred to as the plaintiff. The person against whom the suit is filed is referred to as the defendant. In domestic cases, the complainant is the petitioner, and the person against whom the case is filed is the respondent.

The trial progression of civil actions is as follows:

Filing of a complaint
Filing of an answer
Discovery proceedings
Motions filed relating to discovery matters
Pre-trial proceedings
Trial by judge or jury
Opening statements
Plaintiff's presentation of evidence
Defendant's presentation of evidence

Plaintiff's rebuttal case
Closing arguments
Jury instructed
Deliberations
Verdict

3.8.2 Jurisdiction and Venue

The plaintiff's lawyer decides where to file the case. For a judge to have authority to decide on a case, it must have jurisdiction over the person or property involved.

Venue refers to the county or district within U.S. territory where the lawsuit is to be tried. The lawsuit venue is set by statute, but sometimes it is necessary to change it, particularly if a case has widespread publicity which could negatively affect the defendant's trial.

3.8.3 Discovery

In preparation for the trial, both sides engage in discovery. This is the formal process of exchanging information between the parties about the witnesses and evidence they will present at trial.

A common method of discovery in civil suits is to take depositions. A deposition is an out-of-court statement given under oath. It is to be used at trial in the form of a written transcript, a videotape, or both.

3.8.4 Pre-Trial Conferences

Judges hold pre-trial conferences with lawyers for several purposes. One type is status conference, used by judges to establish a time limit for concluding all pre-trial activities, and to set a tentative date for trial.

Judges and lawyers can also review the evidence and clarify the issues in dispute. At pre-trial conferences, judges may encourage settling cases. Lawyers usually appear at these hearings and try to agree on undisputed facts. Such agreements are called stipulations.

3.8.5 Pre-Trial Procedures in Criminal Cases

The process may be different depending on the severity of the crime. The more serious crimes are felonies, such as robbery, assault with a deadly weapon, and sexual assault. Misdemeanors are less serious crimes, such as simple assault, driving while intoxicated, and trespassing, punishable with fines, probation, or a term of incarceration of less than a year, usually in a local jail. Traffic violations and petty misdemeanors are usually punishable with fines.

These procedures follow the general pattern of civil cases except for a few variations, depending on the gravity of the crime.

3.8.6 Bringing the Charge

Charges are brought against an individual in one of the following ways (charging documents):

- Through an indictment voted by a grand jury.

- Through the filing of information by a prosecutor, also called county, district or state's attorney.

- Through the filing of a criminal complaint by another individual, which is basically a petition to the D.A. asking them to initiate charges.

- Through a <u>citation</u> by a police officer for minor traffic offenses.

The charging document must tell the time, date and place that the criminal offense allegedly took place, and the details of the crime itself.

3.8.7 The Grand Jury, Indictment, and Information

Grand juries are used in the federal system and in most states, but only about half the states use grand juries to bring charges for felony cases.

The grand jury is a body of citizens usually including more than 12, often up to 23 jurors.

(Trial jurors, on the other hand, 12 jurors or less. They are called petit jurors)

Like trial jurors, grand jurors are often selected from voter registration or driver's license registries. They are summoned by the court to serve for a specific period of time. They do not have to agree unanimously to issue an indictment, though state law often requires that two-thirds or three-quarters of the jurors vote to indict.

Grand juries are also appropriately called <u>accusing juries</u>.

The purpose of the grand jury is not to decide whether the defendant is guilty or innocent. It is to determine whether there is sufficient evidence to bring a person to trial.

In states where prosecutors often bring charges without the involvement of a grand jury, the prosecutor files a document called *information* against the defendant, and at a preliminary hearing, a judge or magistrate takes on some of the grand jury's responsibilities in determining whether there is sufficient evidence to charge the suspect with a crime.

Unlike trials, grand jury proceedings are characterized by secrecy in order to encourage witnesses to speak freely without fear of retaliation or threats. It also protects the individuals being investigated in case that the evidence is considered insufficient and an indictment is not issued. Defense attorneys or judges do not have a presence in grand jury sessions since normal rules of evidence do not apply.

3.8.8 Arrest

Once a grand jury has returned an indictment or a prosecutor has filed an information, a judge or a magistrate will issue a warrant for the arrest of the person charged, unless they are already in custody without a warrant. In this case, law enforcement officials may detain the suspect for no more than 48 hours. They may not hold the suspect beyond this time without a first appearance or arraignment hearing before a judge or a magistrate.

3.8.9 Pre-Trial Court Appearances - Regarding Misdemeanors and Felonies

Step 1

- In Florida, the Initial Appearance (or First Appearance) is the defendant's very first court meeting, typically within 24 hours of arrest, to be informed of charges, rights —including the right to trial and to counsel (one is appointed if defendant is indigent), and to discuss bail or pretrial release conditions.

- At the initial appearance, the defendant does not enter a plea.

- The judge sets the amount of bail.

- Key Point: The defendant should avoid arguing about the facts of the case, since any statements they make could be used against them.

The matter is set for a <u>preliminary hearing</u>—to establish if a crime has been committed and if there is probable cause to believe that the defendant committed the crime alleged in the complaint.

Regarding felony cases, an additional preliminary hearing step may be added as an extra safeguard, given the more serious nature of the charges.

Bail

Bail is the amount of money that defendants must pay to be released from custody while awaiting trial. It is not a fine. It is not intended as a form of punishment. Its purpose is simply to ensure that defendants appear for all pre-trial hearings and trial at which their presence is required. Sometimes, bail comes with a no-contact order regarding the victim.

The judge may release defendants <u>on their own recognizance</u>, that means, they do not have to pay bail, they are released on the promise that they will appear for all their hearings.

Step 2

- A <u>Preliminary hearing</u> is an adversarial proceeding that takes place later in the legal process. The purpose of this hearing is to enable the prosecution to demonstrate to the judge that there is sufficient evidence to believe that a crime has been committed and that the defendant is responsible. If the judge finds sufficient probable cause, the case proceeds toward trial.

- If the prosecutor fails to meet this burden of proof, the case may be dismissed.

- This hearing is scheduled after the initial appearance, typically within 14-21 days.

- The judge or prosecutor reads the charges to the defendant, and informs the defendant of their constitutional rights, including their right to trial, to remain silent, and to counsel.

- If the defendant will have counsel, a plea of not guilty will be entered, and a trial date will be set along with additional pre-trial conference dates.

- There are three pleas available: guilty, not guilty, and no contest (or nolo contendere).

- A plea of no contest is equivalent to a guilty plea, except that the defendant does not directly admit guilty. The sentence is the same for the pleas of guilty and no contest.

- The defendant enters a plea.

- If the defendant pleads guilty, or no contest, they will have a future date for sentencing, or the judge will impose a sentence immediately according to the severity of the offense.
- Key Point: It's an opportunity for the defense to demonstrate either that there is no probable cause, or that the evidence was obtained illegally.

Plea Bargaining

Many criminal cases are resolved out of court through negotiation between both sides. This process is known as plea bargaining or negotiation of a plea. In some cases, prosecutors may be able to drop charges in exchange for a guilty plea to a lesser offense, without court approval. "Other alternatives are also possible in the criminal justice system. Many states encourage diversion programs that remove less serious criminal matters from the full, formal procedures of the justice system. Typically, the defendant will be allowed to consent to probation without having to go through a trial. If he or she successfully completes probation – e.g., undergoes rehabilitation or makes restitution for the crime – the matter will be expunged (removed) from the records." Law & the Courts, volume II

3.9 The Trial Process, in Criminal and Civil Cases

3.9.1 Criminal Law Versus Civil Law

It is important to touch on these differences because civil actions and criminal proceedings are two separate legal processes with some similarities.

Criminal Law	Civil Law
Crime as public wrong	Tort as private wrong
Punishment as incarceration or death	Punishment as compensation
Government as prosecutor	Injured person as plaintiff
Proof: Beyond a reasonable doubt	Proof: Preponderance of evidence

*Table taken from CliffsNotes, online study guides. The Nature of Criminal Law

- In criminal cases, the trial process ensures that both the prosecution and the defense have the opportunity to present their case. The prosecution attempts to prove the defendant's guilt, while the defense seeks to establish reasonable doubt.

- In civil cases, the process is very similar; the plaintiff attempts to prove the defendant is liable for damages. Below is a more detailed breakdown of the trial process:

3.9.2 Jury Selection

If the defendant opts for a jury trial, the process begins with the selection of a jury. The attorneys will question potential jurors to make sure they are fair and not biased.

The Jury Pool

- In either a civil or criminal case, the jury for the trial is chosen from a list of potential candidates known as a <u>venire</u>, or <u>jury pool</u>, which has been compiled by the court.

- Juries of between six and twelve citizens are selected from the venire. The size of the jury varies from state to state, depending to some extent on the type of case being tried.

- In some states, alternate jurors are selected to replace jurors who may become unavailable for serious reasons. They hear all the evidence, but they do not participate in deliberations unless they need to replace an original juror.

- The attorneys for both sides conduct questioning of the potential jurors, and this is known as <u>voir dire</u> (to speak the truth).

- If either lawyer believes that a juror has preconceived ideas about the case, they can ask the judge to dismiss that juror <u>for cause</u>. For example, a juror can be dismissed for cause if they are a close relative of one of the parties. Dismissals for cause can be unlimited.

- In addition to challenges for cause, each attorney has <u>a limited number of peremptory challenges.</u> These challenges allow a lawyer to excuse a potential juror without stating a cause because of a belief that the juror will not serve the best interest of the lawyer's client. Peremptory challenges cannot be used to discriminate on the basis of race or sex.

- Once the jury is selected and sworn in to try the case, it is <u>empaneled</u>, and they take their seats in the <u>jury box</u> to hear the case. The judge then instructs them not to discuss the case with outsiders or with each other (until deliberations). In general, jurors do not have the right to ask questions of the witnesses, but some judges allow them to submit questions in writing for the judge and lawyers to consider.

- Jurors are permitted to take notes under certain rules such as: the notes never leave the room, they are not shared with other jurors until deliberations, they are collected by the bailiff at the end of the proceedings and destroyed.

3.9.3 Opening Statements

- Each side's attorney gives an overview of their case, outlining the evidence they will present and the issues on which they want the jury to focus.

- The opening statements must be limited to facts that will be proven by the evidence and cannot be argumentative.

- The trial begins with the opening statement of the party that brought the case to court—the government in a criminal prosecution or the plaintiff in a civil action. This party must prove their case in order to prevail. The defense attorney then follows with their opening statement.

3.9.4 Types of Evidence

- There are two types of evidence: direct and circumstantial (or indirect) evidence.

- Direct evidence consists of eyewitness accounts, a confession, or a weapon.

- Circumstantial evidence suggests a fact by inference, such as the appearance at the scene of a crime, testimony that suggests a connection with a crime, or physical evidence that suggests criminal activity.

- The two types of evidence are equally valuable.

3.9.5 Direct Examination

- The prosecutor in criminal court or the plaintiff in civil court starts the presentation by calling witnesses. The questions asked are direct examinations. This may elicit both direct and circumstantial evidence.

- Witnesses qualified in a particular area are called expert witnesses.

- In general, attorneys may not ask <u>leading questions</u> of their own witnesses. These questions suggest expected answers. Example: "Isn't it true that you saw Marcia waiting across the street before the children arrived?"

- The opposing counsel may raise <u>objections</u> for a variety of reasons under the rules of evidence. For example, objections may be raised to questions that call for an opinion or conclusion from a witness, or to questions that require an answer based on <u>hearsay</u>.

- Hearsay is what the witness says they heard another person say. Generally, hearsay is not acceptable in court, although there are some exceptions.

3.9.6 Sustain/ Overrule

After an objection, the judge either <u>sustains</u> or <u>overrules</u> the objection. If it is sustained, the attorney must rephrase the question or ask a different question.

If the objection is overruled, the witness answers the question.

3.9.7 Cross-Examination

- Once the plaintiff's or government's lawyer has finished questioning a witness, the defendant's lawyer may then cross-examine them.

- Cross-examination is generally limited to matters raised during the direct examination.

- Leading questions may be asked during cross-examination since its purpose is to test the credibility of statements made during the initial (direct) examination. Another reason for allowing leading questions is that the witness is usually questioned by a lawyer who did not originally call them, so they are likely to resist any untrue suggestions.

- During cross-examination, the attorney may attempt to challenge the witness's ability to identify or recall or try to impeach the witness or the evidence. In this context, <u>impeach</u> means to call into question the credibility of the witness or the evidence. This may be achieved by highlighting prejudice or bias on the part of the witness, such as their relationship with one of the parties or their interest in the outcome of the case. Witnesses may be asked if they have ever been convicted of a felony or a crime involving dishonesty, or <u>moral turpitude</u> since this is relevant to their credibility.

3.9.8 Motion for Directed Verdict (Civil) / Motion for a Judgement of Acquittal (Criminal)

- Once the plaintiff or government has presented their evidence, the lawyer will announce that the state/the defense rests. The jury leaves the courtroom.

- <u>The defendant's lawyer in a civil case has the option of making a motion for a directed verdict</u>. The attorney argues that their client's liability has not been proven by the <u>preponderance of the evidence.</u>

- <u>In a criminal trial, the defendant's lawyer can submit a motion for a judgement of acquittal (JOA),</u> on the grounds that the prosecution has failed to prove the necessary elements of its case.

- In both types of cases, the lawyer asks the judge to rule in favor of the defendant.

- If the judge grants the motion, the case is over and the defendant wins.

- If the judge denies the motion, the defense is given the opportunity to present its evidence.

3.9.9 The Defense's Case

- In a criminal case, the defense witnesses may or may not include the defendant. As the Fifth Amendment of the US Constitution protects against self-incrimination, the prosecution cannot require the defendant to testify or speculate about why the defendant has chosen not to testify. The jury will be instructed not to consider the fact that the defendant does not take the stand.

- The defense presents evidence in the same way as the plaintiff or the state. In return, the plaintiff or government has the right to cross-examine the defense's witnesses.

Permission is granted for redirect and re-cross-examination.

3.9.10 Rebuttal

Once the defense has concluded their case, the plaintiff or the government may present rebuttal witnesses or evidence to contradict that presented by the defense.

3.9.11 Sidebars or Conferences

The judge may invite both lawyers to approach the bench to speak to them, or the lawyers may approach the bench on their own. These are called bench conferences or sidebars and are conducted away from the jury's hearing because they might draw unfounded or unfair conclusions from what they hear.

Once all the evidence has been presented and the jury has left the courtroom, either party may request a directed verdict. If the motion is granted, the trial ends then and there. If not, the presentation of evidence is complete, and the case can be submitted to the jury.

3.9.12 Closing Arguments

- Before closing arguments, the judge tells the lawyers which instructions they intend to give to the jury. In their closing arguments, the lawyers may refer to the jury instructions and relate them to the evidence.

- In their closing arguments, or summations, the lawyers discuss the evidence and the inferences drawn from it.

They cannot discuss issues outside the case or evidence that was not presented.

- The lawyer for the plaintiff or the government goes first and refers to the evidence showing how they proved their case to prevail. Then the defense follows and usually answers statements made by the prosecution or the plaintiff; defects in the case are highlighted and the facts that are favorable to their client are summed up.

- Then the prosecution may make one final appeal, a rebuttal in response to the defense's statements.

3.9.13 Jury Instructions

- The judge reads the instructions to the jury. This is referred to as the judge's <u>charge to the jury.</u>

- The judge's role is to explain the relevant laws to the jury and provide guidelines on how to apply them to the facts of the case in their deliberations.

- The judge will explain the standard of proof that the jury should apply to the case: *beyond a reasonable doubt* for criminal cases, *and preponderance of evidence* for civil cases.

- The jurors are to base their conclusions on the evidence presented in the trial. The jurors determine the facts and reach a verdict within the guidelines of the law as provided by the judge.

3.9.14 Mistrials

- These are trials that are not completed successfully. They are terminated and declared invalid before the jury returns a verdict or the judge renders a decision in a nonjury trial.

- Among other reasons for mistrials are:

- ➤ A fundamental error that is prejudicial to the defendant and cannot be remedied by providing the jury with appropriate instructions (for example, if the prosecutor makes highly improper remarks during their summation).

- ➤ <u>Juror misconduct</u> can include having contact with one of the parties, considering evidence not presented in the trial, or conducting independent investigations, for example.

- ➤ The jury is in a state of <u>deadlock</u>, which means it is unable to reach a verdict.

- Either side may make a motion for a mistrial. The judge will or will not grant the motion.

- The principle of double jeopardy would not apply if a defendant has to be tried again due to a mistrial.

3.9.15 Jury Deliberation

- In a criminal trial, the jury retires to the jury room and will deliberate in private to decide whether the defendant is guilty or not guilty. They elect one of the jurors as the foreperson or presiding juror. Once they have reached a unanimous verdict, the judge will announce it. In Florida, all criminal cases require a unanimous verdict, that is, all jurors must agree upon the same verdict.

    "In civil cases, jury decisions should be unanimous wherever feasible. A less-than-unanimous decision should be accepted only after jurors have deliberated for a reasonable period of time and if concurred in by at least five-sixths of the jurors."
    Principles for Juries and Jury Trials, page 6, www.uscourts.gov

- If the jury cannot come to a decision by the end of the day, the jurors may be sequestered or secluded from contact with other people. They will not be allowed to read or view reports of the case being tried.

- If the jurors cannot reach a decision, the case results in a hung jury, leading to a mistrial. The case is not decided, and it may be tried again at a later date before a new jury. Alternatively, the plaintiff or the prosecutor may decide not to pursue a new trial.

3.9.16 Verdict

Either the foreperson or the court clerk may make the announcement.

Usually, the lawyer for the losing party may ask that the jury be <u>polled</u>. This means that each juror will be asked to confirm their agreement with the decision. Once the decision has been read out and accepted by the court, the jury is dismissed and the trial is over.

Once the judge enters a judgment on the decision, which will be filed in public records, the decision of the jury becomes final.

*This section is mainly based on Law & the Courts, volume II, pages 16 – 28.

3.10 The Post-Trial Process

3.10.1 Sentencing

In a criminal case, a sentence will be imposed by the judge if the defendant is found guilty, and this may include imprisonment, fines or other penalties. The judge will set a date for sentencing. In summary:

- A judge orders a <u>presentence investigation (PSI)</u> after conviction of a defendant and before a sentence hearing.

- It is written by the corrections officer, a probationary officer or any officer who supervises the defendant.

- "During the PSI, the officer conducts an extensive interview with the defendant to discuss the individual's history and background, including childhood experiences, family factors, education, employment, criminal history, finances, physical and mental health, and alcohol or drug use. The officer verifies the information through contacts with family members, friends, employers, and community members. The officer also gathers documentation that can provide useful information for the court, such as court and school records, military service and employment records, documents related to the defendant's finances, medical and employment history. The officer also conducts a thorough review of the criminal offense, including interviews with law enforcement officers and victims." (uscourts.gov)

- A PSI helps the court in determining an appropriate sentence according to the sentencing guidelines.

- Post-trial motions and appeals can be filed by the defense. These vary from state to state.

- Post-trial motions may include a Motion for a new trial.

3.10.2 Types of Sentences

Regarding criminal cases, a Concurrent Sentence involves serving multiple prison sentences for different crimes at the same time. The duration of the sentence is determined by the longest individual sentence.

For example:

If a defendant is convicted of armed robbery and possession of a firearm and receives concurrent sentences of three years for armed robbery and two years for firearm possession, they will serve a total of three years. The sentences are served simultaneously.

A <u>consecutive sentence</u> occurs when prison sentences for multiple crimes are served one after another. For example, following the example above,

If a defendant is convicted of armed robbery and possession of a firearm and receives <u>consecutive sentences</u> of three years for armed robbery and two years for firearm possession, they will serve a total of five years in prison.

3.10.3 Appeals

With regard to criminal or civil appeals:
- An appeal must be legally permissible – there must be an alleged significant error in the trial.

- In a civil case, either party may appeal to a higher court. In most states, the only person who has the right to appeal in a criminal case is the defendant.

- Criminal defendants convicted in state courts have an additional safeguard. Once they have exhausted all their rights of appeal at state level, they can file a <u>writ of habeas corpus</u> in federal courts to demonstrate that their federal constitutional rights were violated.

- <u>An appeal is not a retrial or a new trial</u>. Appeals courts do not usually consider new witnesses or new evidence. Cases are usually appealed based on errors in the trial procedure or the judge's interpretation of the law, and the appeals court merely reviews the trial transcript to determine if errors occurred.

- The party appealing is known as the appellant, or occasionally, the petitioner. The other party is called the appellee, or the respondent.

- The appellate court determines whether errors were made in the application of the law by the lower court. It will generally only reverse a decision if there has been an error of law. However, not every error of law is grounds for reversal.

*This section is mainly based on Law & the Courts, volume II, pages 28, 29.

3.11 The Juvenile Justice System

3.11.1 Three Categories

The jurisdiction of the juvenile court includes three categories of youths:

- **Delinquents**—youths who commit acts that, if committed by adults, would be considered criminal, including misdemeanors and felonies.
- **Status offenders**—youths who commit acts that, if committed by an adult, would not be defined as criminal (for example: truancy, running away from home, and curfew violations).
- **Dependent and neglected children**—youths who are deprived and in need of support and supervision.

"**Age** is the most important obvious criterion separating the juvenile court from the adult criminal court. State laws vary in the minimum and maximum age restrictions. Under common law, the minimum age for holding a person accountable for criminal behavior is seven. Maximum age is the age when a person is defined as an adult and no longer subject to the authority of juvenile court. Most states set the maximum age at 17 years of age or below."

*This section is based on CliffsNotes.com/study-guides/criminal-justice, A separate System for Juveniles

3.11.2 Criminal Procedure

1. Referral:

The process begins when a juvenile is referred to the system, typically by law enforcement, schools, or social service agencies.

2. Investigation:

The juvenile's situation is investigated to determine the nature of the offense or the reasons for their involvement.

3. Detention:

If deemed necessary, the juvenile may be held in detention, and booked, until the next court hearing. The child must appear before a judge for a detention hearing within 24 hours of being taken into custody. At this hearing, the judge will decide whether to release the child, place them under home detention or detain them in a juvenile facility.

4. Court Proceedings:

The juvenile appears in court, where the charges are explained, and a decision is made about the case.

- **Arraignment**: At arraignment, the child is formally informed of the charges and enters a plea (guilty or not guilty).

- **Adjudicatory Hearing**: If the child pleads not guilty, the case proceeds to an adjudicatory hearing, which is similar to a trial in adult court. In Florida, juvenile trials are typically bench trials, meaning the judge, not a jury, determines guilt or innocence.
  *The term adjudication in juvenile court means that a juvenile has been found guilty of an offense. It is equivalent to a finding of guilt in adult criminal court.

5. Disposition:

- A disposition hearing is held for a juvenile who has been found guilty. It is the equivalent to a sentencing hearing in adult criminal court.

- The court will then determine the appropriate disposition or course of action, which may include probation, home detention, community service, counseling, or other interventions.

- When it comes to disposition in juvenile justice, the penalties or interventions are oriented towards rehabilitation rather than punishment.

6. Supervision:

If the juvenile is placed on probation, they will be assigned a probation officer who will oversee their progress and ensure they comply with the terms of their probation.

7. Reentry:

Once the juvenile has completed their sentence or probation, they may be provided with support to transition back into the community.

(The section above was taken from sources across the web and www.flcourts.gov)

3.12 More Legal Terms

Recidivism (return to crime)

Recidivism refers to the tendency of a convicted criminal to reoffend after serving their sentence. It is often defined as the reoffending of an offender, which can include being rearrested, reconvicted or reincarcerated.

Dismissal with prejudice

Dismissal with prejudice means a court case is permanently dismissed. The plaintiff cannot refile the same claim against the same defendant. It's a final judgment on the matter. This concept is applicable in both civil and criminal courts.

Dismissal without prejudice

A dismissal without prejudice means a court case is closed for now, but the plaintiff or prosecutor can refile it. The case to be brought again.

This concept is applicable in both civil and criminal courts.

Prosecutorial Misconduct

Prosecutorial misconduct is defined as the illegal or unethical actions of a prosecutor during a criminal case, often with the intention of influencing the jury or obtaining a conviction through improper means. This can encompass the withholding of evidence, the presentation of false information, or the utilization of inappropriate arguments to the jury. Such misconduct has the potential to violate a defendant's constitutional rights and compromise the fairness of the trial process.

Vacate

In the context of legal proceedings, the term *vacate* is understood to signify the annulment or setting aside of a prior court order or judgment. The process is fundamentally concerned with the reversal or cancellation of a decision that has been made by the court. This can be achieved by way of a motion to vacate, whereby one party requests that the court reconsider and overturn its previous ruling.

Writ of Certiorari

A writ of certiorari is an order issued by a superior court that directs a subordinate court to submit the documentation of a case for review. Its primary function is to facilitate the process of petitioning for review of a lower court decision, a practice that is most commonly associated with the U.S. Supreme Court. In essence, the appeal is a request for the Supreme Court to hear the case.

In essence, a writ of certiorari is primarily used to appeal a lower court's decision to a higher court, such as the Supreme Court.

The U.S. Supreme Court is not bound by the requirement to grant a writ of certiorari. The courts have the discretion to select cases for hearing, and the decision to grant the writ is made on a case-by-case basis.

Codicil

A codicil is defined as an addition or supplement that either explains, modifies or revokes a will or part thereof.

Example: Albert has remembered him in a <u>codicil</u> to this will.

3.13 Examples of Court-Related Terms and Usage Test Sections. The following are examples of the court-related terms and usage sections that you will find in the written exam. The prompts follow the exam model created by the National Center for State Courts (NCSC).

Section 6: *Sentence Completion.* Items 76-111 consist of unfinished sentences that are likely to be heard in the court environment. Please select from the list of four words or phrases the option that <u>most appropriately</u> completes the sentence

Example: An accessory is

A. a person who aids or contributes to the commission of a crime.
B. one who knowingly, voluntarily, and intentionally unites with the principal offender in the commission of a crime.
C. the generic name for the defendant in a criminal case.
D. the person who sets up a trust.

(A is the option that most appropriately completes the sentence.)

Section 7: *Court-Related Questions.* Items 112 through 121 consist of questions regarding court-related topics. The candidate is instructed to select from a list of four choices the one that is the <u>best</u> answer.

Example: What does the term "trier of fact" refer to?

A. *The jury or the judge must make findings of fact*

B. *The jury must make findings of fact*

C. *The judge must make findings of fact*

D. *The judge must make rulings of law*

(A is the option that most appropriately answers the question.)

<u>Section 8: Sequence.</u> Items 122 through 125 consist of questions about the proper sequence of events in court-related situations. Please select from a list of four choices the option that correctly describes the order in which the events should occur.

Example: Choose the correct sequence of events involving the Miranda rights.
A. Arrest, Miranda rights, interrogatory
B. Arrest, interrogatory, Miranda rights
C. Interrogatory, arrest, Miranda rights
D. Miranda rights, interrogatory, arrest

(A is the option with the correct sequence of events.)

3.14 Key Points: Concepts That You Need to Know

- Steps in processing a criminal case
- Fourth, Fifth, Sixth, Eighth, Fourteenth Amendments
- Case law
- Miranda rights
- Felonies, misdemeanors, infractions
- Mens rea, actus reus, concurrence
- Pre-trial, trial, post-trial processes
- Types of sentences
- Criminal procedure in juvenile justice system

Chapter 4: Ethics and Professional Conduct

Florida Court interpreters abide by the Code of Ethics established by the Supreme Court of Florida. The following principles govern our professionalism:

4.1 Professional Conduct

- Court interpreters must uphold the integrity of the profession by maintaining respectful behavior in all assignments. Their conduct should reflect ethical standards that foster trust in judicial proceedings.

Example Scenario:

An interpreter arrives early to a high-profile civil trial and greets courtroom staff, attorneys, and bailiffs with calm professionalism. During the hearing, she maintains focused eye contact, a poised demeanor, and neutral body language, even while interpreting emotionally charged testimony. At one point, an attorney tries to rush the process and interrupts the interpreter mid-sentence. Rather than responding defensively, the interpreter politely requests, in the third person, to finish conveying the full statement for accuracy, using respectful language and tone. The interpreter may say:

"Your Honor, may the interpreter be permitted to complete the interpretation for accuracy?"

Or

"Your Honor, may the interpreter kindly be allowed to finish interpreting the full statement for accuracy?"

This interaction not only preserves the interpreter's composure and credibility but also demonstrates respect for everyone involved—including the speaker, the listener, and the judicial process itself. Such behavior strengthens public trust in interpreters as impartial officers of the court.

4.2 Accuracy and Completeness

- Court interpreters must faithfully render the full meaning of every spoken statement without omissions, additions, or alterations. Precision in terminology and nuance is essential to uphold fairness and ensure that the record reflects exactly what was said.

Example Scenario:

During a preliminary hearing, a defendant says in Spanish, "No me acuerdo exactamente, pero creo que estaba allí." The phrase translates to "I don't remember exactly, but I think I was there." The interpreter, thinking she can help clarify, renders it as *"He remembers being there."*

Although well-intentioned, this subtle shift alters the speaker's degree of certainty, replacing ambiguity with affirmation. Such imprecision can significantly affect how testimony is perceived by the judge and attorneys. The interpreter's duty is not to streamline—but to convey the speaker's exact meaning of words, tone, and level of certainty with fidelity.

> ➤ In the event of an error, the interpreter should promptly acknowledge it by stating either *"The*

interpreter stands by her interpretation" or "The inter-preter stands corrected."

- The interpreter must accurately convey the speaker's emotional tone without imitating gestures or physical mannerisms.

Example Scenario:

During a heated sentencing hearing, the defendant yells, "This is unfair! You're punishing me for something I didn't do!" while pointing aggressively and shaking their head. The interpreter's task is to faithfully convey the emotional tone—anger, urgency, defiance—through vocal delivery alone.

Rather than gesturing wildly or raising their arms to mimic the defendant's physical outburst, the interpreter uses controlled vocal emphasis: maintaining volume, inflection, and emotional intensity consistent with the speaker's tone—while remaining physically neutral and professionally composed.

This approach preserves fidelity without overstepping the interpreter's role or distracting the court with performative behavior.

- Court interpreters must render every spoken utterance on the record during proceedings, including—but not limited to—jury instructions and statements by defendants or other participants. Interpreters are strictly prohibited from altering, omitting, or embellishing any part of the official discourse, even if such a request comes from a court officer or any other party. In such instances, interpreters must immediately inform the requesting party that the action constitutes a violation of the Code of Ethics and firmly decline to comply.

Example Scenario:

During a sentencing hearing, a court officer discreetly tells the interpreter, "The defendant mumbled something just now—no need to repeat it. It wasn't important." The interpreter, however, clearly heard the defendant say, "This is so unfair. You'll regret this."

Recognizing that every utterance on the record must be interpreted faithfully, the interpreter declines the officer's suggestion. They respond professionally:

"I understand your concern, but the statement is part of the official record. As per the Code of Ethics, I'm required to interpret everything said in the courtroom without omission or alteration."

The interpreter then proceeds to render the defendant's exact words into the target language, preserving tone and nuance while remaining neutral and composed.

4.3 Representation of Qualifications

- Interpreters must accurately represent their credentials, skills, and certifications, neither exaggerating nor misrepresenting their expertise.

Example Scenario:

A bilingual individual is eager to gain courtroom experience and submits an application to interpret during a misdemeanor trial. He lists "certified court interpreter" on his resume, assuming that passing a general language proficiency exam qualifies him. However, he has not yet earned official certification recognized by the state or jurisdiction.

During the trial, his lack of specialized training becomes apparent, resulting in interpretation errors and confusion for the defendant. When questioned, the interpreter admits to overstating their credentials.

This misrepresentation not only jeopardizes the fairness of the proceedings but may lead to disciplinary action and reputational harm. Ethical interpreters must always state their qualifications accurately and accept assignments only within their verified scope of expertise.

(This example was created purely to make a point. Ideally, only certified court interpreters should interpret in trials.)

> ➢ Interpreters should accept only assignments they are qualified to perform, ensuring competent service and protecting the integrity of the profession.

4.4 Impartiality and Avoidance of Conflict of Interest

- Interpreters must remain neutral and refrain from any behavior that suggests bias toward any party in a proceeding.

Example Scenario:

During a family court hearing, an interpreter develops empathy for a non-English-speaking parent who seems distressed and underrepresented. In an attempt to comfort him, the interpreter smiles warmly, offers unsolicited words of encouragement in their native language between testimony, and subtly softens the tone when interpreting the judge's remarks.

Although well-intentioned, these actions compromise the interpreter's impartiality. Even small gestures—like tone shifts, off-the-record remarks, or visible sympathy—can signal favoritism and undermine trust in the process. The interpreter must instead maintain a calm, professional demeanor and strictly interpret what is said, without embellishment or personal engagement.

- Interpreters must avoid situations where personal, financial, or professional interests could compromise—or appear to compromise—their objectivity.

Example Scenario:

An interpreter is assigned to a criminal case where one of the defense attorneys is a close personal friend. Even if the interpreter believes they can remain impartial, their relationship could give rise to the *appearance* of bias—especially if legal outcomes are contested.

In this case, the interpreter must disclose the relationship to the presiding officer and request to be recused from the assignment.

- If an interpreter is also a licensed attorney, they must not serve in both roles within the same case to prevent ethical conflicts and preserve the integrity of each profession.

Example Scenario:

A bilingual attorney is invited to serve as a court interpreter in a case unrelated to their law practice. However, after reviewing the case materials, he realizes the proceedings touch on legal matters he has previously worked on.

Even if he is qualified linguistically, serving as both legal counsel and interpreter in any capacity would pose a clear ethical conflict. To preserve professional integrity, the attorney must decline the interpreter's role for that case.

- During proceedings, interpreters must refrain from engaging in personal conversation with parties, witnesses, jurors, attorneys, or anyone connected to the case—including friends or relatives of any party—except when necessary to fulfill their official interpreting duties.

Example Scenario:

An interpreter is assigned to a civil litigation case and notices that one of the jurors is a distant cousin she hasn't seen in years. During a recess, the cousin approaches to say hello. The interpreter responds warmly and begins catching up in the hallway. A court officer overhears the exchange and reports it to the judge, raising concerns about the interpreter's impartiality.

Even though the conversation was friendly and unrelated to the case, interacting personally with a juror—or anyone connected to the proceeding—violates ethical standards. The interpreter should have politely declined the interaction and maintained distance to preserve professional neutrality.

- Before accepting an assignment, court interpreters must disclose to all parties and presiding officials any prior involvement—personal or professional—that could reasonably be viewed as a conflict of interest. Such disclosure must exclude any privileged or confidential information.

Example of how to handle this:

"Before proceeding, the interpreter would like to disclose that he previously interpreted for Mr. Dueñas in a separate civil matter.

He has had no further professional or personal involvement with the case or the parties beyond that role. The interpreter leaves it to the presiding officials to determine whether his participation in this assignment presents a concern."

- Interpreters must not accept assignments in which their compensation is tied to the outcome of the case. Payment should be based solely on services rendered, not influenced by verdicts, settlements, or any result of the proceeding.

Example Scenario:

An interpreter is offered a contract by a party in a civil lawsuit, promising bonus compensation if the client wins the case. Accepting this arrangement would violate ethical standards, as it creates a financial incentive that could compromise the interpreter's neutrality and professionalism.

- Interpreters must inform the presiding officer of any personal bias or prior experience that could affect their neutrality in a proceeding. For instance, an interpreter who has survived sexual assault may choose to be excused from interpreting cases involving similar subject matter to maintain emotional distance and professional objectivity.

Sample Statement to the Presiding Judge:

"Your Honor, the interpreter respectfully requests to be excused from this matter as she cannot maintain emotional neutrality and professional objectivity. She asks for your understanding and appreciate the opportunity to uphold the integrity of the role."

4.5 Confidentiality and Restriction of Public Comment

- Court interpreters must preserve the confidentiality of all information acquired during the course of their duties. They are strictly prohibited from discussing case details, parties, or proceedings outside the official context—even in general or anonymized terms. Public commentary, including social media posts, interviews, or casual conversations that could compromise privacy or the perception of impartiality, must be avoided entirely.

Example Scenario:

After interpreting in a sensitive juvenile dependency hearing, an interpreter attends a professional conference and casually mentions how "a recent case really pulled at her heartstrings" and shares vague details about a child's testimony—even without names or locations. Later, another conference attendee realizes he was involved in that exact proceeding and raises concerns.

Even though the interpreter did not disclose names, referencing case content in a public or semi-public setting breaches confidentiality and could undermine trust in the legal process. Similarly, posting online comments such as, *"Some cases just stay with you..."* alongside courtroom-related hashtags or images—even without specifics—can create an appearance of impropriety or bias.

- Interpreters are also prohibited from granting interviews to the media, regardless of the nature or outcome of the pro-ceeding.

Example Scenario:

An interpreter is hired to facilitate communication in a sensi-tive immigration hearing where confidential details are dis-cussed, including past asylum claims and familial safety con-cerns. Weeks later, the interpreter is approached by a journalist seeking insight into courtroom trends and mentions this specific case.

Even without revealing names, the interpreter must decline to share any case details, as doing so would breach confidential-ity and erode trust in the process.

4.6 Professional Demeanor

- Court interpreters must conduct themselves with respect, self-control, and discretion at all times. Their appearance, behavior, and communication should reflect the serious-ness of the judicial process and reinforce confidence in their role as impartial language professionals.

Example Scenario:

An interpreter is scheduled to work in a high-stakes civil trial. She arrives early, dressed in court-appropriate attire—conserva-tive, clean, and professional—and greets courtroom staff with quiet courtesy. Throughout the proceeding, she remains poised and attentive, avoiding side conversations, emotional reactions, or distracting movements. When asked a procedural question by an attorney during a recess, she responds briefly, staying within the bounds of her role and deferring to the judge for any decisions outside the scope of interpretation.

In general, even in moments of stress or confusion, the interpreter maintains composure. They also maintain clear communication. This reinforces their credibility. It also reinforces the court's confidence in their impartiality. Their presence signals the seriousness and respect of the proceedings.

4.7 Scope of Practice

- Court interpreters must strictly adhere to their defined role, which is to facilitate accurate communication between parties in the judicial process. They must not offer legal advice, express personal opinions, or engage in activities beyond interpretation—even if asked by a litigant or attorney.

If they have to sight translate a document, they do not explain its content.

Example Scenario:

During a family court hearing, an interpreter is handed a custody agreement to sight translate for a parent with limited English proficiency. As he begins reading the document aloud in the target language, the parent interrupts and asks, "So does this mean I'll lose my visitation rights?"

Despite the emotional weight of the question, the interpreter does not answer. He maintains his role by continuing to render the document exactly as written, without any commentary or legal explanation. After completing the sight translation, he respectfully refers the parent to his attorney for clarification.

Later, the same attorney casually asks the interpreter what he thinks the judge will decide. The interpreter politely declines to speculate, explaining that his role is limited to language interpretation, not legal analysis or personal opinion.

4.8 Assessing and Reporting Impediments to Performance

- Interpreters must continuously monitor their ability to perform during assignments and immediately report any physical, emotional, or situational impediments that compromise accuracy or impartiality. If at any point their performance is hindered—due to fatigue, illness, emotional distress, or conflict—they are obligated to notify the presiding officer and request appropriate accommodation or relief.

Example Scenario:

An interpreter is midway through an all-day criminal trial involving emotionally graphic testimony. By early afternoon, she begins to feel lightheaded and mentally fatigued, noticing lapses in concentration and slower response time. Realizing that continued interpretation under these conditions risks compromising accuracy, the interpreter discreetly alerts the judge, stating:

"Your Honor, the interpreter is experiencing fatigue that's affecting her ability to interpret with full precision. She respectfully requests a brief recess or replacement to maintain the integrity of the proceedings."

The judge grants a break and arranges for a standby interpreter to take over if needed.

(The ideal scenario for lengthy hearings is team interpreting where the interpreters switch every 30 minutes or so.)

Another Statement for Disclosure

"Your Honor, the interpreter respectfully requests to be excused from this proceeding due to [state reason—fatigue, illness, emotional discomfort, or conflict of interest]. He believes continuing may impact the accuracy and impartiality of his interpretation."

Example Scenario

Imagine you're halfway through an assignment when a witness mentions an event that triggers a personal memory. You feel your concentration slipping. What should you do?

Ethical Response: Take a moment to assess your ability to continue objectively. If you feel you cannot, politely request to speak with the judge privately to disclose your concern in professional terms.

Key Points to Consider:

- To maintain mental and physical acuity, interpreters should request periodic breaks as needed during proceedings.
- Before accepting an assignment, they must inquire about the nature of the case to assess readiness.
- If specialized terminology arises, the interpreter should ask for a brief recess to review the subject matter; if substantial research is required, this must be communicated to the presiding officer.
- Interpreters should discourage requests to interpret audio or video recordings. However, if directed to proceed, they

may do so only after clearly stating on the record that they cannot certify the accuracy of the rendition.

The interpreter may say:

> *"Your Honor, the interpreter respectfully wishes to state for the record that he cannot certify the accuracy of the interpretation of this recording."*
>
> Or
>
> *"Your Honor, for the record, the interpreter would like to clarify that she cannot guarantee the accuracy of the interpretation of this audio/video recording."*

See elaborate information on this point at the end of this section.

Use this guide before and during proceedings to ensure you're fit to perform at your best:

Assessment Point	Reflective Prompt	Action if Concern Arises
Physical wellness	Am I alert, rested, and free from illness?	Request relief if performance may falter
Emotional clarity	Can I remain composed and focused throughout?	Pause and assess emotional readiness
Impartiality	Can I interpret without personal bias?	Disclose conflict or concern
Environmental conditions	Is noise, seating, or visibility affecting accuracy?	Notify presiding official

Preparation	Have I received sufficient case context or materials?	Request clarification or support

Or:

1. Are you physically and mentally fit to interpret today?

No: Notify presiding officer; request relief

Yes: Proceed with assignment

2. Do you know the nature of the case and feel qualified?

No: Inquire for details before accepting

Yes: Accept with confidence

3. Are you encountering unfamiliar terminology?

No: Request a brief recess to resolve it

Yes: Proceed with confidence

4. Requires deeper study?

No: Continue interpreting

Yes: Inform presiding officer

5. Asked to interpret audio/video recording?

No: Proceed normally

Yes: Express concern. You may say:

"Your Honor, the interpreter would like to respectfully clarify that interpreting recorded audio or video material during

proceedings is not within the scope of real-time court interpreta-tion. This task typically requires transcription and translation out-side the courtroom setting, to ensure accuracy and proper review. The interpreter is happy to assist in any authorized manner once that process is complete."

If the judge insists, you may proceed, but you must state on the record that the interpreter cannot certify their interpretation. (See the examples above for guidance on how to address the is-sue to the judge.)

4.9 Duty to Report Ethical Violations

- Court interpreters have an ethical obligation to report any known or suspected violations of professional standards by fellow interpreters, legal personnel, or others involved in the proceedings. This duty upholds the integrity of the judicial process and ensures that breaches—whether in-tentional or inadvertent—are addressed appropriately through official channels.

Example Scenario:

While interpreting during a felony arraignment, Interpreter A observes Interpreter B repeatedly omitting portions of the de-fendant's statements and altering the tone of witness testimony. Interpreter A also overhears Interpreter B discussing personal opinions about the case with a court clerk during a break.

Although Interpreter A is not officially assigned to monitor In-terpreter B's performance, these observations raise serious con-cerns about impartiality and fidelity to the role. Understanding their ethical obligation, Interpreter A documents the incidents and submits a confidential report to the court's interpreter coordinator and administrative authority, citing concerns and requesting a formal review.

By taking this step through official channels—and avoiding gossip, judgment, or speculation—Interpreter A upholds the integrity of both the profession and the proceedings, ensuring that any misconduct is addressed responsibly and transparently.

- If an interpreter becomes aware of information indicating imminent harm to any individual, they must promptly report it to the appropriate judicial authority.

Example Scenario:

While interpreting during a pre-trial interview, the interpreter hears a defendant say—in their native language—"As soon as this is over, I'll make sure they pay for this. I know where they live." The statement is made in a quiet aside, not part of the formal questioning, but the interpreter understands that it suggests a potential threat against another party in the case.

Because the comment indicates possible imminent harm, the interpreter must report it to the presiding judge or appropriate court authority immediately—even if the threat wasn't directed at them, and even if it was spoken outside the official record. Silence in this case would risk endangering lives and violating ethical duty.

4.10 Professional Development

Court interpreters have a responsibility to pursue ongoing education and skill enhancement to maintain excellence in their work. This includes staying current with changes in legal terminology, interpretation techniques, cultural competency, and ethical standards, ensuring they meet evolving demands within the judicial system.

Professionalism is a continuous journey, not a static credential.

4.11 Examples of Ethics and Professional Conduct Questions. The directions follow the format of the written exam created by the National Center for State Courts (NCSC).

Section 9: Professional Conduct Questions. Items 126 and 127 consist of questions about the appropriate course of professional conduct an interpreter should take. Please select from a list of four alternatives <u>the best</u> solution or course of action.

Example: Which of the following should the interpreter avoid in order to maintain professional conduct?

A. Demonstrating friendliness to all parties
B. Presenting the appearance of bias toward any of the parties
C. Maintaining cultural awareness during interpretation
D. Clarifying terminology when requested

(B is the option that most appropriately answers the question.)

Section 10: Scenarios: Items 128 through 135 consist of brief scenarios describing situations an interpreter might encounter while interpreting in the courts that would pose ethical or professional problems. Please select from a list of four alternatives <u>the best</u> solution or course of action.

Example: In an emotionally charged case, a witness uses racial slurs, graphic descriptions, and hate speech. What should you do?

A. Inform her supervisor of the situation
B. Despite personal discomfort, she must render the message faithfully and without censorship
C. Inform the judge that she cannot use profane language
D. She feels so bad that she thinks she should leave the courtroom

(B is the correct answer.)

4.12 Key Points. The Ten Ethical Principles

- Professional conduct
- Accuracy and completeness
- Representation of qualifications
- Impartiality and avoidance of conflict of interest
- Confidentiality and restriction of public comment
- Professional demeanor
- Scope of practice
- Assessing and reporting impediments to performance
- Duty to report ethical violations
- Professional development

ANNEX 1

Advancing Your Practice:

You may use this annually to assess your progress and set growth goals:

Focus Area	Action Item	Completion Date
Terminology Update	Review of recent legal terminology changes	
Ethics & Standards	Revisit Code of Ethics; check for updates	
Technique Refinement	Practice sight translation, simultaneous, and consecutive modes	
Cultural Competency	Explore sociocultural nuances impacting interpretation	
Continuing Education	Attend workshops, webinars, or courses	
Peer Feedback	Request skill review from colleague or mentor	

Language Expansion	Strengthen lesser-used working languages	
Tech Familiarity	Learn new court software or remote interpreting tools	

ANNEX 2

Career Stage Study Map

Tailor learning goals based on experience level:

Stage	Primary Goals	Suggested Resources
Entry-Level	Build core ethics, terminology, and courtroom procedure	Intro courses, mentorship, glossaries
Mid-Level	Hone technique, address real-world challenges	Ethics scenarios, peer workshops
Seasoned Interpreter	Specialize, mentor others, stay current with trends	Advanced seminars, leadership training
Expert Mentor	Expand impact through teaching or policy contribution	Training design, ethics committee service

Bibliography / References

This bibliography includes the foundational sources that have shaped the ethical insights, practical scenarios, and instructional tools shared in this book. Selected to support mentees, educators, and professionals, these references reinforce the values of impartiality, accuracy, and responsibility in court interpretation. Each entry offers a pathway to deeper understanding and continued growth within the judicial process.

Reference List (APA Style)

Books

Law & the Courts. (n.d.). *Volumes I, II*. [American Bar Association]

Government & Legal Resources

Florida Courts. (n.d.). *Official website*. Retrieved June, 2025, from https://www.flcourts.gov
U.S. Courts. (n.d.).

Federal judiciary overview. Retrieved May, June, July 2025, from https://www.uscourts.gov
Florida Courts. (n.d.). *Code of Professional Conduct: Florida Rules for Certification and Regulation of Spoken Language Court Interpreters*. Retrieved July 8-10, 2025, from https://www.flcourts.gov

Educational & Legal Content

CliffsNotes. (n.d.). *Criminal Justice Study Guides*. Retrieved May through July, 2025, from https://www.cliffsnotes.com/study-guides/criminal-justice
Lumen Learning. (n.d.). *Introductory criminal justice courses*. Retrieved June 10, 2025, from https://courses.lumenlearning.com
Nolo. (n.d.). *Legal topics for consumers and professionals*. Retrieved June 10, 2025, from https://www.nolo.com
Thomson Reuters Legal. (n.d.). *Legal research and insights*. Retrieved June 15, 2025, from https://legal.thomsonreuters.com

Career & Legal Culture

Climb the Ladder. (n.d.). *Career guidance for legal professionals*. Retrieved June 20, 2025, https://www.climbtheladder.com
BPI Law. (n.d.). *Legal blog and professional commentary*. Retrieved June 15, 2025, from https://www.bpi-law.com

AI-Supported Resources

Various sources. (2025). *AI-generated overviews compiled across the web*. Synthesized by Microsoft Copilot.

Resources for Court Interpreters

The following organizations and websites provide reliable, up-to-date information on legal procedures, interpreter ethics, judicial conduct, and courtroom education. These sources can support court interpreters in deepening their knowledge and staying aligned with best practices in the field.

Legal Institutions & Professional Associations

- **American Bar Association**
  www.americanbar.org and www.abanet.org
  Offers resources on legal education, professional standards, and policy updates that interpreters may encounter in legal settings.
- **National Center for State Courts**
  www.ncsc.org
  Provides model codes, interpreter services guidelines, and tools for state-level legal professionals.
- **Florida State Courts**
  www.flcourts.gov
  Includes Florida's interpreter registry, certification rules, and the official Code of Professional Conduct for court interpreters.
- **United States Courts**
  www.uscourts.gov
  Offers federal court information, interpreter policies, and access to judiciary resources across all district levels.

Associations for Interpreters and Translators

- **National Association of Judiciary Interpreters and Translators (NAJIT)**
  www.najit.org
  Provides continuing education for judicial interpreters and translators. Organizes annual conferences, publishes the quarterly newsletter *Proteus*.
- **American Translators Association (ATA)**
  www.atanet.org
  Provides continuing education for interpreters and translators in general. Organizes annual conferences, publishes the monthly ATA *Chronicle* and other publications, provides certification for member translators and offers several divisions and special interest groups for members. It is a worldwide organization.
- **American Association of Interpreters and Translators in Education (AAITE)**
  www.aaite.org
  Provides professional development series, articles and publications of interest for interpreters and translators.
- **Association of Translators and Interpreters of Florida**
  www.atifonline.org
  It is a Florida chapter of ATA, it offers professional development activities, monthly gatherings, and more.

Legal Education & Public Access Tools

- **Oyez Project**
  www.oyez.org
  Multimedia archive of U.S. Supreme Court cases—excellent for understanding case law, oral argument structure, and legal terminology in context.

- **Street Law**
  www.streetlaw.org
  Legal education for the public and students—especially useful for interpreters working in community outreach or educational programs.

Check the terms you already know,

even if some of them are not mentioned in this book. You may write your own notes next to each term.

- adjudication hearings
- administrative rules
- adversary system
- affidavit
- aggravating/ mitigating circumstances
- alibi
- allocation
- amendment
- appeal
- arraignment
- arrest
- arson
- attorney-client privilege
- bail/bond
- bench trial
- bench/jury trial
- beyond a reasonable doubt
- bond/bail
- boot camps
- burden of proof
- burglary
- capital crime
- challenges, peremptory challenge
- charging document
- common law/case law
- complaint
- concurrence

- concurrent vs consecutive sentences
- constitution
- conviction
- criminal vs civil
- cross-examination
- curfew
- custody
- death penalty
- defendant
- delinquent
- detention hearings
- deterrence
- direct examination
- dismiss with/without prejudice
- disposition
- district attorney
- diversion
- double jeopardy
- DUI
- eavesdropping, bugging
- eighth Amendment
- electronic monitoring
- evidence
- exclusionary rule
- ex-parte
- fact-finder
- felonies
- felonious crimes
- first and second degree murder
- first appearance hearing
- forcible vs statutory rape

- fourth and fifth Amendments
- grand jury
- guidelines
- guilty plea
- hearsay
- hit and run
- house arrest
- hung jury
- in lieu of
- indictment
- information
- infractions
- initial appearance
- innocent until proven guilty
- insanity
- investigation
- jails
- jury pool
- jury trial
- larceny-theft
- lenient sentence
- mediation
- mens rea
- miranda warnings
- misdemeanor
- mitigate
- moot trial
- motion for discovery
- motion to dismiss
- motion to suppress
- municipal ordinances

- nolle prosequi
- nolo contendere/no contest
- opening/closing statements
- pardon
- parens patriae
- parole
- penalty phase
- petit jurors
- physical evidence
- plea bargaining
- prejudice
- preliminary hearing
- preponderance of evidence
- pretrial motions
- prisons
- probable cause
- probation
- prosecutorial discretion
- prosecutorial misconduct
- PSI report
- recidivism
- robbery
- aggravated assault
- ROR
- search
- seizure
- self-incrimination
- sentencing
- shoplifting
- sixth amendment
- speedy trial

- standard of proof
- statutes
- strikes
- suborning perjury
- testimonial evidence
- the right to counsel
- tort
- trial court
- truancy
- vacate
- vehicular homicide
- victim impact statement
- voir dire
- warrant
- white collar crimes
- wiretapping
- writ of attachment

www.ingramcontent.com/pod-product-compliance
Lightning Source LLC
Chambersburg PA
CBHW051634120626
46551CB00014B/2075

* 9 7 9 8 9 9 3 0 1 0 1 6 8 *